Ages 8-9

DISNEY LEARNING

PIXAR

Magical Adventures in
Third Grade

W9-AAC-598

Carson Dellosa Education
Greensboro, North Carolina

This workbook belongs to:

_____

Disney **LEARNING**

Published by
Carson Dellosa Education
PO Box 35665
Greensboro, NC 27425 USA

Printed in the USA • All rights reserved.   ISBN 978-1-4838-5869-2
06-057211151

Contents

Dear Learner,

This workbook encourages you to practice essential skills alongside your favorite Pixar characters. It is designed to reinforce foundational concepts learned in school and boost your skills and confidence in reading, writing, and math.

Examples and Practice: Pixar characters are learning partners. They provide examples to help teach you core concepts!

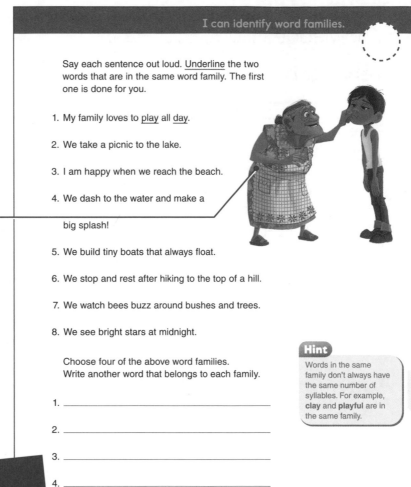

I can identify word families.

Say each sentence out loud. <u>Underline</u> the two words that are in the same word family. The first one is done for you.

1. My family loves to <u>play</u> all <u>day</u>.

2. We take a picnic to the lake.

3. I am happy when we reach the beach.

4. We dash to the water and make a big splash!

5. We build tiny boats that always float.

6. We stop and rest after hiking to the top of a hill.

7. We watch bees buzz around bushes and trees.

8. We see bright stars at midnight.

Choose four of the above word families. Write another word that belongs to each family.

1. _____

2. _____

3. _____

4. _____

Hint

Words in the same family don't always have the same number of syllables. For example, **clay** and **playful** are in the same family.

© Disney/Pixar

17

Congratulations
to
_____!
Print your name.
You have completed this workbook. You're a superstar!

Completion Certificate: Find the certificate in the back of this book. Fill in this certificate after you have completed this workbook.

I can identify word families.

. Underline the two
 word family. The first

day.

beach.

Did You Know?

Consonant **blends** are two or three consonants that work together to make a blended sound. In a blend, you can hear each consonant sound, like **fl** in **fly** and **str** in ~~street~~.

Hint

Words in the same family don't always have the same number of syllables. For example, **clay** and **playful** are in the same family.

I Can: Each lesson includes an "I can" statement. It indicates what you are able to do and can also be a learning target or goal.

Reward Stickers: To conclude each lesson, a reward sticker can be placed in the dashed red circle. Find stickers in the back of this book. Use the reward stickers as motivation to finish the lessons.

Did You Know?: Find more information about topics in the lessons in this pop-up box.

Hint: Find additional support for challenging topics in this pop-up box.

Bonus Activities: Suggestions are provided beginning on page 206 to further develop and foster your understanding of subject areas important to school success.

Glossary: Definitions, background information, and explanations of **black bolded** terms can be found in the glossary.

Answer Key: Sample answers for activities are provided, where necessary, at the back of the book.

Happy Learning!

Count 'em!

The name **Mike** has one **syllable**. The name **Sul / ley** has two syllables. The word **Mon / stro / po / lis** has four syllables!

A Say each word. Draw slashes to separate each word into syllables. Write the number of syllables in each word. The first one is done for you.

1. mon/ster __2__   2. child/ren __2__

3. scare __1__   4. fac/to/ry __~~2~~ ✓3__

5. me/chan/i/cal __~~3~~ ✓4__   6. col/lec/tor __3__

7. clo/set __2__   8. scream __1__

9. friend/ship __2__   10. build/ings __2__

11. team/mates __2__   12. night/time __2__

13. worked __~~2~~ ✓ 1__   14. scar/ing __2__

15. se/cre/tive __3__   16. en/e/my __3__

DidYou Know?

Words have parts called **syllables**. Every syllable has a vowel sound. The number of vowel sounds you hear in a word is the number of syllables.

Hint

Clap each syllable as you say a word. The claps will help you hear and count the syllables.

B Write a sentence using at least three two-syllable words.

_____

_____

_____

6

C Fill in the table.

1. Sort these words into the table.

machine   conveyor   company

~~light~~   ~~Boo~~   energy

worker   ~~friends~~   ~~safe~~

~~Randall~~   helper   passageway

One Syllable	Two Syllables	Three Syllables
safe	helper	energy
Boo	Randall	company
light	worker	passageway
dump	machine	conveyor
sole	← friends	
	1 syllable	

2. Draw slashes to separate each two-syllable and three-syllable word into syllables.

3. Add your own word to each column in the table.

Consonant Crew

Like Lightning McQueen's pit crew, some consonants work as a team.

A Complete each of the following words, which all have a consonant **blend**. Say the word. Listen for the blend.

1. scr   squ   str   ~~str~~ing

2. sm   fl   cr   ~~sm~~ile

3. fr   sk   spl   ~~spl~~ash

4. ng   nt   rk   pare~~nt~~

5. st   nd   bl   du~~st~~

6. tr   scr   fr   ~~fr~~uit

7. gl   gr   cr   ~~gl~~ue

8. lp   ng   rst   fi~~rst~~

B Underline the consonant blends in these sentences.

1. Guido is a blue forklift.

2. Luigi and Guido are best friends.

3. Luigi's shop has many tools, like screwdrivers and ratchets.

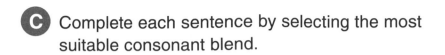

C Complete each sentence by selecting the most suitable consonant blend.

spr   dr   rk   sp   scr   tr

1. Lightning ~~spr~~ _dr_ eams of winning races.

> **Hint**
> Try each of the blends with each word to find a match.

2. Racing takes practice and hard wo_rk_____.

3. On dirt racetracks, the cars _spr____ay mud everywhere.

4. Smokey helps Lightning get ready to race on

   the _____tr__ack.

5. The cars race at a very high ____sp__eed.

6. Sometimes tires make a ____scr__eeching sound.

D Write a word for each of the consonant blends.

str   fr   cl

1. ___street_____

2. ___fret_____

3. ___clue_____

Consonant Combo

Bo Peep rounds up her missing sheep.

Round up some consonant **digraphs** in these activities.

A Say each word and listen for the digraph. Circle the digraphs in each word.

1. (ch)air

2. wrap

3. those

4. when

5. bush

6. wash

7. whale

8. laugh

9. sock

10. cheese

11. ship

12. neck

13. shop

14. shark

15. wish

16. child

Did You Know?

Consonant **digraphs** are two consonants that work together to make one sound, like **sh** in **sheep**. Some digraphs go at the beginning of words. Some digraphs go at the end.

B These digraphs are special. They can appear at the beginning or at the end of a word. Write two words for each digraph.

1. ch_ain_ ___ar___ch

2. sh_oe_ ___wa___sh

3. th_ough_ ___fif___th

C Add a consonant digraph to each word to solve each riddle.

th   ck   wh   sh   ch   wr

1. The opposite of right: _wr_ ong

2. Do this to a soccer ball: ki_ck_

3. Body part under your mouth: _ch_ in

4. The color of Bo Peep's sheep: _wh_ ite

5. Brush these to prevent cavities: tee_th_

6. These have fins and scales: fi_sh_

D Read the poem below. Underline the consonant digraphs.

> Bo Peep's sheep are lost. Will they start to cry?
>
> All the toys want to help—they have to try!
>
> But wait, what have they found?
>
> The sheep are in a basket, safe and sound!

Did You Hear That?

Miguel's Abuelita has forbidden him to play and listen to music, but Miguel still loves listening to music. Let's listen to some letter sounds!

A Say the sound made by the two **purple** letters: f**or**bid. Circle the words that have the same sound as the **or** in **forbid**.

d**oor** photo guitar

st**ore** perf**orm** roar

music mem**ory**

time m**ore**

B Say the sound made by the two **purple** letters: guit**ar**. Circle the words that have the same sound as the **ar** in **guitar**.

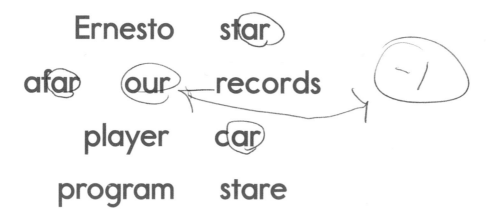

Ernesto st**ar**

af**ar** our records

player c**ar**

program stare

C Say each word.

Circle the word that does not make the same sound as the **purple** letter or letters. The first one is done for you.

1. o**ff**er   (highway)   phone   tough

2. **th**is   then   feather   (otter)

3. l**a**te   raise   (stack)   eight

4. bri**ng**   (young)   engine   something

5. f**i**ne   kite   (try)   (kid)

6. boo**k**   (know)   candle   like

7. **c**ircle   seed   cell   (call)

8. dr**ea**m   (wet)   week   eagle

9. **p**late   pack   apple   (phone)

10. **g**rass   giggle   (giant)   grow

> **Hint**
>
> A **limerick** is a fun poem with five lines. The rhyming pattern is AABBA.

D Complete the limerick using the **purple** words.

There once was a boy named ___Miguel___ ,

Who could play the guitar quite ___well___ .

When Abuelita heard him ___play___ ,

She wanted the songs to go ___away___ !

Will Miguel give music a ___farewell___ ?

farewell

away   well

Miguel   play

Winner or Whiner?

Vowels can have a short sound or a long sound.

The **u** in **Junior** is a long vowel. The **u** in **Hudson** is a short vowel.

Say their names to hear the difference.

A Say each word in the left-hand column. Identify whether the sound of the **purple** letter in each word is long or short. Circle your choice.

1. gate   long   short

2. best   long   short

3. smile   long   short

4. coach   long   short

5. mud   long   short

6. crash   long   short

7. Smokey   long   short

8. loss   long   short

9. unit   long   short

10. McQueen   long   short

11. track   long   short

12. fit   long   short

Did You Know?

A vowel is usually short when it is the only vowel in a word (r**e**d). A long vowel will often "say its name" (c**a**ke, l**i**ke, p**o**le). When a word ends in a silent **e**, the first vowel is usually long (t**i**le). When two vowels "go walking, the first one does the talking" (t**e**am).

B Say each word that Natalie Certain and Chick Hicks use in their broadcast. Is the **purple** letter in each word a long vowel or a short vowel? Sort the words into the correct column of the chart.

tires   speed   crash

dodge   truck

spin   pole

screech   race

rude   uniform   sped

Long Vowel	Short Vowel

All in the Family

Miguel has a big family. Words have families, too! Words in a family also share similar features.

A Match each word on the left to its word family.

1. quick

   > mold   unfold   sold

2. marigold

   > plate   gate   crater

3. blame

   > mail   pail   rail

4. jump

   > goat   throat   coat

5. float

   > lump   thump   bumper

6. hesitate

   > frame   game   same

7. trail

   > flick   thick   pick

B Say each sentence out loud. <u>Underline</u> the two words that are in the same word family. The first one is done for you.

1. My family loves to <u>play</u> all <u>day</u>.

2. We take a picnic to the lake.

3. I am happy when we reach the beach.

4. We dash to the water and make a

   big splash!

5. We build tiny boats that always float.

6. We stop and rest after hiking to the top of a hill.

7. We watch bees buzz around bushes and trees.

8. We see bright stars at midnight.

C Choose four of the above word families. Write another word that belongs to each family.

Hint

Words in the same family don't always have the same number of syllables. For example, **clay** and **playful** are in the same family.

1. _____

2. _____

3. _____

4. _____

Sight and Sound

Mike and Sulley are practicing for the Scare Games. They need to look and sound scary!

Words aren't scary, but pay attention to how they look and sound.

A In each row, <u>underline</u> the words that are alike.

1. eight	freight	trust	weight
2. truth	peel	booth	tooth
3. mess	Mike	miss	moss
4. puppy	purple	pop	puck
5. try	muddy	cry	fry
6. veil	mail	ceiling	male

Did You Know?

Recognizing how words are alike can help you read new words. However, words may be alike in the way they look, but sound different (**tour** and **sour**). They can also be alike in the way they sound, but look different (**Sulley** and **Celia**, which both begin with the **s** sound).

B In each row, (circle) the letter or letters that make the same sound.

1. clean   mean   bean

2. men   bet   them

3. slip   sleek   slide

4. skate   plate   date

5. crush   dish   shy

6. photo   final   form

7. rang   sing   clung

8. moan   groan   loan

9. boo   soup   tool

10. scare   hare   mare

C Write five more words in the **scare** word family.

scare

Climb for New Words

The Green Army Men use a rope to climb the dresser to look for Hamm. They could also use a ladder to climb up the dresser.

Another kind of ladder is a word ladder. A word ladder can be used to make words.

A Start at the bottom rung. Change one letter to make a new word for each rung.

1.

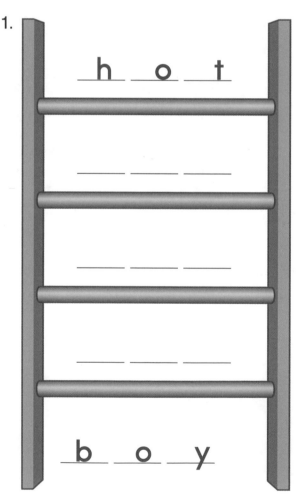

h o t — not cold

____ ____ ____ — a small jump

____ ____ ____ — the opposite of bottom

____ ____ ____ — an object children play with

b o y — a young male child

2.

_____ _____ _____ _____ _____   the opposite of give

_____ _____ _____ _____ _____   a sticky strip of material

_____ _____ _____ _____ _____   another word for a story

_____ _____ _____ _____ _____   an event when you can buy items cheaper

_____ _____ _____ _____   a young or old man

_____ _____ _____ _____   the hair on a horse's head

_____ _____ _____ _____   belonging to me

_____ _____ _____ _____   when you eat a meal

d   i   v   e _____   to jump headfirst into the water

-Er, -Ar, -Or?

Miguel wants to be a guitar player. He meets Héctor in the Land of the Dead. Héctor asks for a favor. He wants his photo on Miguel's family altar.

Notice that **player**, **favor**, and **altar** all have a similar **er** sound.

A <u>Underline</u> the words ending in **-er**, **-or**, and **-ar** endings in each sentence.

1. Dante is a fast runner and a good hunter.

2. Miguel is a visitor in a very different world.

3. Ernesto de la Cruz is a believer in the power

   of music.

4. Miguel and Ernesto have a similar taste in music.

5. Maybe Miguel will be a popular music

   conductor someday.

6. What Miguel learns is to always remember his family.

7. Mamá Coco thinks of her father when she hears

   Miguel sing.

8. Héctor is the creator of many of Ernesto's songs.

Did You Know?

There is no easy rule to know when to use **-er**, **-ar**, and **-or** endings. (The **-er** ending is used more than the other two.) Knowing when to use these endings just takes practice!

B Add an **-er**, **-ar**, or **-or** to complete the word in each sentence.

1. Last night at dinner, we had a very funny wait_____.

2. Some shirts have a coll_____ around the neck.

3. We need another act_____ for our play.

4. Friends tell me I am a good listen_____.

5. My aunt is a brave firefight_____.

6. I eat my salad with oil and vineg_____.

7. I will become an invent_____ and help the world.

8. The reflect_____ on my bike is cracked.

9. I am not a great swimm_____.

10. At this store, everything costs one doll_____.

C Draw a (circle) around the words using **-er**, **-or**, and **-ar** that do not make an **er** sound.

Hint

The **-er** ending is usually used for someone doing an action (**trucker**, **teacher**). The **-or** ending is usually used for words ending in **-ate**, **-ct**, **-it** (**calculate**, **conduct**, **visit**). When adding **-er** to a word with a short vowel that ends in a consonant, double the consonant (**thin – thinner**).

star   sugar   floor

fear   father   solar

editor   anger   soccer

poor   guitar

Grrr-eat Base Words

Bo helps Woody find Forky. You could call her helpful.

Help is the **base word** of **helpful**.

A Draw a ⬭circle around the base word in each set. Write the base word on the line.

1. dislike   unlikely   likeness

_____

2. remove   movers   unmoved

_____

3. disagree   agreement   agreeable

_____

4. helpful   unhelpful   helper

_____

5. unpack   packer   repacking

_____

6. reopen   opener   unopened

_____

B Find the word in each sentence that has a prefix or a suffix. <u>Underline</u> the base word within that word.

1. Rex's roar could be stronger.

2. He is scared of frightful things.

3. He speaks nervously when he is afraid.

4. He is often hiding under things.

5. His friends don't like to hurt his feelings.

6. They treat him with kindness.

7. Woody came to untangle Rex.

8. Rex is hardly ever unhappy.

C Follow the instructions to invent new words! Define your words.

1. Add a suffix to a base word. _____

Definition: _____

2. Add a prefix to a base word. _____

Definition: _____

3. Add a prefix and a suffix to a base word. _____

Definition: _____

Preview Prefixes

Cruz Ramirez and Lightning McQueen do a lot of prerace work.

Pre- is a prefix that means "before." **Prerace** means "before the race."

A Match the base word with the correct prefix.

1. dis   kind

2. un   historic

3. re   obey

4. pre   tell

B Put the prefix and the base word together. Complete the table.

Prefix	Base Word	Word	Definition
dis	like		
un	lock		
re	fill		
pre	mix		

C Choose the correct prefix to complete the word.

dis- un- re- pre-

1. After stalling, Lightning has to _____ start his engine.

2. Lightning and Cruz practice hard in the _____ season.

3. Trainers and racers sometimes _____ agree about how to get ready for a race.

4. Lightning is _____ happy about arguing with Cruz.

5. Cruz's worries _____ appear when she hits the track.

D Choose three of the words you completed in Part A, B, or C. Use each in a sentence.

_____

_____

_____

_____

How Does It End?

At Monsters University, Sulley makes Mike feel good by telling him that he is fearless.

Fearless is a word that uses the suffix **-less**.

A Choose a suffix or suffixes for each base word. Write the new word(s) on the line.

-less   -ful   -able
-dom   -ship

1. free _____

2. comfort _____

3. friend _____

4. need _____

5. break _____

6. play _____

7. value _____

8. power _____

9. care _____

10. champion _____

Hint

-less means "without"

-ful means "full of"

-able means "able to be"

-dom means "state of being something" or "an area"

-ship means "showing a special quality of something"

B Complete each word by choosing the correct suffix.

-less   -ful   -able

-dom   -ship

1. The royal family lives in the king_____.

2. My scraped knee is pain_____.

3. The alien boarded his star_____.

4. I sometimes feel help_____ when I don't read directions.

5. The TV show is very enjoy_____.

C Unscramble the words. Add a suffix. Write the word in the last column.

Scrambled Word	Unscrambled Word	Suffix	Word
hpel			
beatuy			
ignk			
rivred			
mebrem			

A Nice, Pleasant, Good, Fine Dog

Dante is a good friend to Miguel. Dante is a **pal**, a **buddy**, a **companion**, a **chum**.

The words in **purple** are all **synonyms** for the word **friend**.

A Match each word to its synonym.

1. teach   difficult

2. journey   instruct

3. challenging   trip

4. brief   like

5. pleased   short

6. enjoy   satisfied

30

B Replace the **purple** word in each sentence with one of the listed synonyms.

races   unhappy

achieve   wonder

1. When Miguel feels **down**, he plays his guitar.

2. Ernesto de la Cruz tells Miguel to **reach** for his dreams.

3. Dante **dashes** through the streets.

4. Miguel is filled with **awe**.

Hint

Use a thesaurus to help you find synonyms.

C Write two synonyms for each word.

1. tiny _____

2. say _____

Yes and No, High and Low

Mike and Sulley are opposites. Mike is small while Sulley is big. Mike is studious while Sulley is carefree. Mike's roar is quiet. Sulley's roar is loud!

Words have opposites, or **antonyms**, too.

A Draw a (circle) around the antonym in each group of words.

1. wrong   right   incorrect

2. indoors   outdoors   outside

3. easy   hard   difficult

4. healthy   sick   well

5. wide   thick   narrow

6. same   different   alike

B Write a sentence using the antonym of each word.

1. dry

_____

2. cheerful

_____

C Complete the puzzle with antonyms for the listed words.

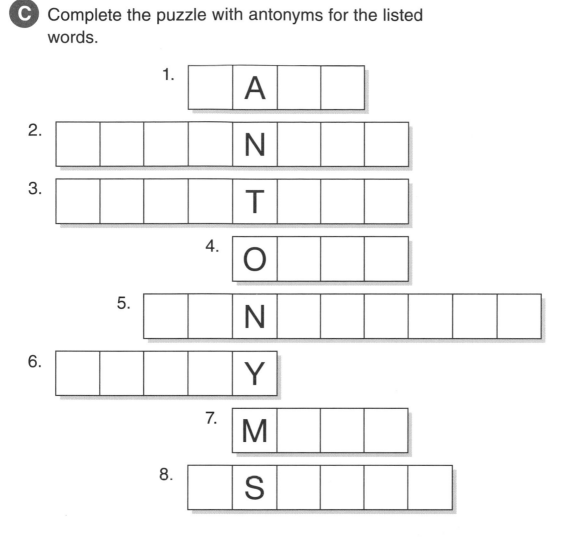

1. A
2. N
3. T
4. O
5. N
6. Y
7. M
8. S

1. short   2. unfriendly

3. boring   4. under

5. nervous   6. rainy

7. few   8. awake

Two for One

It's a special day at the speedway!

Speedway is a compound word.

A Place a check mark beside the cars that have compound words in their name.

_____ Chuck Armstrong   _____ Darrell Cartrip

_____ Kevin Racingtire   _____ Sally Carrera

_____ Billy Oilchanger   _____ River Scott

_____ Kevin Shiftright   _____ Junior Moon

_____ Cal Weathers   _____ Shannon Spokes

_____ Arvy Motorhome   _____ Brent Mustangburger

_____ Bubba Wheelhouse   _____ Darren Leadfoot

> **Did You Know?**
>
> The meaning of a **compound word** is often related to both words (**hailstorm**, **toothpaste**, **cupcake**).

B Draw a (circle) around the compound words.

Put a slash between the two words that make the compound.

racetrack	cheering	speeding
performance	headlight	alongside
compete	zoomed	weekend
thunderous	grandstand	retirement

C These compound words got mixed up. Fix them!

poptub   lightcorn   suitbulb

bathnail   passcase   fingerword

1. pop + _____ = _____

2. light + _____ = _____

3. suit + _____ = _____

4. bath + _____ = _____

5. pass + _____ = _____

6. finger + _____ = _____

D Create compound names for three cars.

1. _____

2. _____

3. _____

We're All for Contractions!

Sometimes, things can be turned into something else. Bonnie took trash and turned it into Forky! Make contractions by turning two words into one.

A Write the contraction made from the two words.

1. is not _____

2. have not _____

3. I am _____

4. you are _____

5. did not _____

6. would not _____

B Write the two words that make up the contraction.

1. we're _____

2. she's _____

3. shouldn't _____

4. there's _____

5. he's _____

C Draw a (circle) around the correct contraction.

1. What is another way to say **it is**?

   it's   mightha've   mightv'e

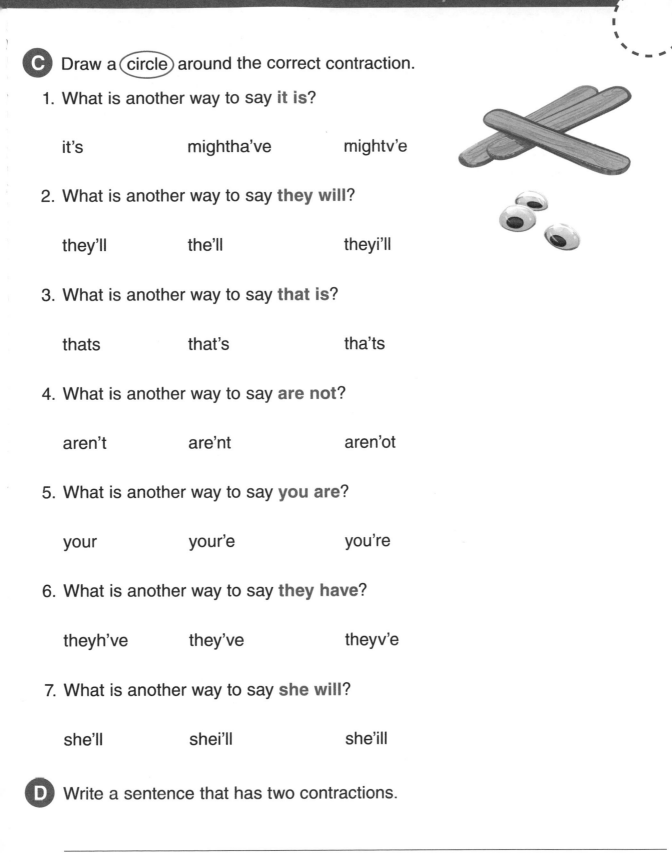

2. What is another way to say **they will**?

   they'll   the'll   theyi'll

3. What is another way to say **that is**?

   thats   that's   tha'ts

4. What is another way to say **are not**?

   aren't   are'nt   aren'ot

5. What is another way to say **you are**?

   your   your'e   you're

6. What is another way to say **they have**?

   theyh've   they've   theyv'e

7. What is another way to say **she will**?

   she'll   shei'll   she'ill

D Write a sentence that has two contractions.

_____

_____

Short and Sweet

Sulley and Mike go to Monsters University (**MU**). After they graduate, they hope to work at Monsters, Incorporated (Monsters, **Inc**.).

 A Match the long form of each word with its **abbreviation**.

1. sec.	Fahrenheit
2. Tues.	February
3. Ave.	Apartment
4. Feb.	Tuesday
5. ft.	Avenue
6. F	feet
7. Apt.	second

B Draw a circle around the correct abbreviation.

1. What is another way to write **September**?

Sep.   Sept   Sept.   Septem.

2. What is another way to write **2 liters**?

2 L   2 Ll   2 LTRS   2 LS

3. What is another way to write **Highway 10**?

Hiw 10   Hwy. 10   hwy. 10   Hiway 10

4. What is another way to write **Wednesday**?

wed   Wednes.   Wen.   Wed.

C Fill in the chart.

Word(s)	Abbreviations
Friday, March 30	
Professor	
20 seconds	
Oozma Kappa	
Thursday	
3 feet	
Sunday, April 1	

Spelling Strategies

Miguel loves to play guitar.

Guitar is a tricky word to spell. You can use rhymes and other memory prompts to help you spell tricky words.

 Read the spelling rules. Write the complete words in the third column. The first one is done for you.

Rule	Rule in Use	Final Words
u after **q**	squ + ad	squad
	qu + een	
when a word ends in a consonant + y, change **y** to **i** when adding an ending, unless the ending is **-ing**	supply + ing	
	happy + er	
if adding an ending that starts with a vowel, drop silent **e** and throw in the towel	race + er	
	trace + ing	
short vowel, consonant, plus a vowel ending—double up the consonant, because it needs some friending	hop + er	
	drop + ing	

Did You Know?

There are sometimes exceptions to spelling rules. For example, if a short vowel is followed by the letter x, the x is not doubled (**fix** – **fixed**).

B Follow the rules in Part A to spell each of these words correctly.

1. Add -**est** to **funny**. _____

2. Spell the opposite of **loud**. _____

3. Add -**er** to **shop**. _____

4. Add -**ous** to **fame**. _____

5. Spell the sound that ducks make. _____

6. Add -**ing** to **win**. _____

C Correct the spelling mistake in each **purple** word.

1. The **daisyes** in the vase are wilting. _____

2. Are the cookies **bakeing**? _____

3. Your **qestions** are important. _____

4. The rabbits are **hoping** all around the yard. _____

5. To make the cake batter, we **mixxed** the sugar and butter first.

_____

6. We saw many cars **raceing** around the track. _____

7. She is **happyest** when her dog is at home. _____

8. The **qeust** to find library books was successful. _____

Cruise by the Pit Crews

Let's hope Lightning McQueen's **brake** pedal doesn't **break**!

The words **brake** and **break** are examples of **homophones**.

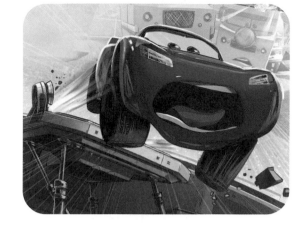

A Read each word. Listen to how it sounds. Write a homophone for each word.

1. mail _____

2. plain _____

3. blue _____

4. aunt _____

5. where _____

6. cheep _____

7. cell _____

8. rap _____

9. waist _____

10. eye _____

B Draw a (circle) around the correct homophone in each sentence.

1. Lightning and Cruz Ramirez practice on a sandy

   beach   beech.

2. The racers drove **threw   through** the woods.

3. Sometimes racers skid **write   right** into tires.

4. Races are sometimes held at **knight   night**.

5. Lightning sometimes flies **passed   past** Cruz.

6. In another race, Cruz easily **beats   beets** Lightning.

7. On the dirt track, the tires **scent   sent** mud flying.

8. Racers love to say, "I **one   won!**"

C Write two homophones for each word.

1. bye _____   _____

2. sow _____   _____

3. too _____   _____

It's Raining Cats and Dogs

Whoa! Sometimes the toys **get in hot water**.

This **idiom** means they get into trouble.

A Use your eagle eye to match the idiom to the correct meaning.

1. a green thumb

make a risky choice

2. a piece of cake

infer, or use clues

3. get a kick out of

good at gardening

4. read between the lines

tell a secret

5. the apple of my eye

really enjoy

6. let the cat out of the bag

the thing I love most

7. gets my goat

very easy

8. hold your horses

plan

9. go out on a limb

wait

10. get all your ducks in a row

is annoying

Did You Know?

An **idiom** is an expression that doesn't really mean what the words say. Idioms are a type of figurative language. They add interest and energy when you speak or write.

B Underline the idiom in each sentence. Write its meaning in the second column.

Idiom	Meaning
1. The toys wait on pins and needles for Bonnie to play with them.	
2. Some toys are on the fence about Forky being one of them.	
3. Bo keeps her chin up when she is facing hard times.	
4. Forky feels like a fish out of water when he's not in the trash.	
5. Woody and Forky are in the same boat when they get lost.	
6. Woody getting lost was a blessing in disguise.	
7. Bo was over the moon that Woody decided to stay with her.	

C Make up your own idiom! Explain what your idiom means. Use it in a sentence.

Idiom: _____

Meaning: _____

Sentence: _____

What's Your Prediction?

Natalie Certain thinks she can predict who will win the next big race. Natalie uses what she already knows and what she can see to make **predictions**.

A Read the title of the text on the next page.

1. Predict what kind of text it will be.

_____ fiction   _____ nonfiction

2. What do you predict the text will be about?

_____

_____

B Read the text. Then, answer the questions.

Go-Kart Kids

Posted by: Amelia Tracy at 7:30 p.m.

Comments (1)   Likes (4)

Welcome to my go-kart blog! I have been go-karting since I was 6. My dad helped me learn. Last summer, we built a go-kart!

I have finished two go-kart races so far. I have some tips if you are new to racing:

1. Always have an adult with you.

2. Always wear a helmet and safety gear.

3. Drive straight for as long as you can.

4. Have a strong grip on the steering wheel.

Have fun on the track!

1. How close were your predictions?

_____

2. What clues did you use to make your predictions?

_____

_____

3. How did you use what you already knew to help you make predictions?

_____

I Know What That's Like!

Stories can mean more to us when we make connections with them.

Mike Goes on a Field Trip

Mike Wazowski is excited to go on a field trip with his class. They are going to Monsters, Inc. Mike has wanted to visit Monsters, Inc. for a very long time.

Mike is the smallest of his classmates. Some of the other students are not nice to him.

They arrive in a big yellow bus and gather around their teacher. She reminds them to behave and look out for each other.

A guide gives them a tour of the Monsters, Inc. building. The guide takes them to the Scare Floor. The guide shows them where scream energy is produced.

Mike is very interested. He bravely watches a Scarer at work.

After the field trip, Mike is excited. Even though Mike may be small, he has big dreams. He knows what he wants to be when he grows up—a Scarer!

Did You Know?

Making connections means thinking about what a story reminds you of in your own life. You can make connections to other books, TV shows, movies, people you know, or real-life events.

Hint

When you read the story, ask yourself questions such as: Have I ever felt like that? Has something like that ever happened to me? Do I know other stories like this? What events, outside my own life, does this remind me of?

A Think about the parts of the story that remind you of something you have experienced. Explain one of your connections.

_____

_____

_____

_____

_____

B What other real-life events, stories, or shows does this story remind you of?

_____

_____

_____

_____

_____

_____

What Are You Telling Me?

A Examine the picture and read the story.
Make inferences about how Mamá Imelda is
feeling. Underline the clues in the text. Draw an
emoji in the margin to show how she feels.

An Autumn Mystery

One crisp morning, Mamá Imelda stands
in a very long line at the Marigold Grand
Central Station. She is getting ready to
leave the Land of the Dead for the first
day of *Día de los Muertos*.

When she finally reaches the front of the
line, she is stopped. "Sorry, *señora*," an
agent says to Mamá Imelda. "No photo on
an *ofrenda*, no crossing the bridge. Next!"

"What?" shouts Mamá Imelda, furiously.
"My family always puts the photo of me
and my daughter on the altar!"

Mamá Imelda stomps over to the
Department of Family Reunions. She
quickly finds a clerk who works there.

Mamá Imelda demands to know why she can't cross into the Land of the Living. Suddenly, out of the corner of her eye, she sees her family and a young boy walking toward her. She recognizes the young boy as her living great-great-grandson Miguel. He is holding an old photo. As they get closer, she can see the familiar faces of a woman and a young girl in the photo Miguel is holding.

"I think I know what happened," Mamá Imelda says crossly.

Hint

To make inferences, ask yourself questions like these: Why is this information here? What do these words tell me? What do the character's words and actions tell me?

B Answer the questions. Explain which clues helped you make this inference.

1. Are many people leaving the Land of the Dead?

_____

_____

2. Did Mamá Imelda's family forget to put her photo on the *ofrenda*?

_____

_____

Why Do You Ask?

Randall sees an article about Boo arriving at Monsters, Inc.

What questions do you think Randall has about the article?

 Write a question Randall might ask before, during, and after reading the article. The table has some examples.

Before: _____

During: _____

After: _____

Before	• What form of text is this? • What do I know about the form? • Who is the author? • What can I tell from the title? Headings? Pictures? • What do I think this text will be about?
During	• What does this part mean? • What does this remind me of? • What do I think will happen next?
After	• What do I think about this text? • What connections can I make to this text? • How does this text affect me?

Did You Know?

Asking questions helps you better understand what you are reading. You also stay more interested in the text.

B Imagine Randall wrote a letter to the newspaper saying children are dangerous. Here is the response the editor might write.

List questions you have before, during, and after reading the text.

> Dear Randall,
>
> Thank you for your letter to our newspaper. It was nice of you to remind us that children are very dangerous.
>
> We also enjoyed reading about how much you like scaring kids. You must work hard at Monsters, Inc. to collect so many screams. Could we interview you to learn more about the Scare Floor?
>
> Please let us know if you are available for an interview. Thank you for your support!
>
> G. R. Rowler
> Editor-in-Chief
> *Monstropolis Horn*

Before: _____

_____

During: _____

_____

After: _____

_____

Who's in the Driver's Seat?

A As you read this story, think about the **point of view**.

My Inspiration

I am Cruz Ramirez, a race car trainer. I don't want to blow my own horn, but I am considered the best in the business. I have seen Lightning McQueen. I know he is out of shape. But I can help him.

I have ways to help Lightning. When he completes practice races, I can track his time and help him improve. I have learned a few new moves myself. I love racing!

Not everyone knows this, but Lightning inspired me to be a racer. One day, I know my dream will come true.

Did You Know?

Stories are told from someone's **point of view**. If a story is told by a character, that is called the first-person point of view (**I am so fast.**). When you read a text from a character's point of view, it can really help you understand how they think and feel. If a story is told by a narrator who is not in the story, it is called the third-person point of view (**She is so fast.**).

1. Who is telling this story?

_____

_____

2. Which words tell you who is telling this story?

_____

_____

3. Is the story written from a first-person point of view or a third-person point of view? How do you know?

_____

_____

B Rewrite Cruz's story from Lightning's point of view. The first two sentences are written for you.

My name is Lightning McQueen. I'm a very famous race car!

_____

_____

_____

_____

_____

© Disney/Pixar

Getting the Message

Some monsters and Boo are in a restaurant. Suddenly, the monsters realize Boo is there. All of the monsters panic and try to get away from Boo. A table is knocked over. Trays and food are flying.

 A Draw a circle around the **main idea**.

Monsters like to eat in restaurants.

The monsters are afraid of Boo.

Boo eats food.

Trays and food are flying.

Did You Know?

The **main idea** tells us what the text is about. To find the main idea, separate the most important idea from the less important details.

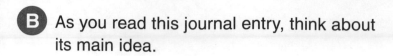

B As you read this journal entry, think about its main idea.

October 16

Today in class, we wrote about what it takes to be a good customer at a restaurant. The most important part of being a good customer is simple: just be polite.

The next time I go to a restaurant, I will make sure to chew my food quietly. I will not throw food or run around while people are eating. I will also treat the restaurant staff nicely. I shouldn't scream and turn over tables if I see something I don't like in the restaurant.

I can't wait to go to a restaurant and practice what I learned today about being a good customer.

Hint

To find the main idea, look for words that are repeated. Look for language that is strong and direct. Ask yourself: What do I think the author really wants me to remember?

1. What is the main idea in this journal entry?

_____

_____

2. What helped you identify the main idea?

_____

_____

Summarizing

Buzz can talk about the solar system forever! He should **summarize** the information so he can help Forky easily understand!

A Read the article. Use the table on the next page to summarize the article.

Our Planet Earth

We live on a planet called Earth. Earth is the third planet of the solar system. The solar system is a collection of the sun, eight planets, and the planets' moons. Earth has many special features that make it different from other planets.

The average temperature on Earth is 57 degrees Fahrenheit. Other planets that are closer to the sun are much hotter. Planets that are farther away from the sun are much colder.

As far as we know, Earth is the only planet in our solar system that has liquid water on its surface all the time. However, scientists are exploring other planets to see if they also have liquid water.

It takes Earth 24 hours to make one full rotation. Other planets take a longer time to rotate. Venus, for example, takes 243 days to make a rotation. The timing of Earth's rotation means that all areas of the planet receive sunlight regularly. Sunlight helps plants and trees grow and produce oxygen.

Did You Know?

A **summary** is a brief statement of the main points of a text in your own words. When you **summarize**, you show that you understand the meaning of what you read.

Hint

Include the most important information in your summary, not just interesting details.

---

1. Title	
2. What is the subject of this article?	
3. Why did the author write this article?	
4. What are three important ideas from this article?	a) b) c)
5. Summarize the article in two sentences.	

When All Is Said and Done

As Miguel leaves Ernesto de la Cruz's tomb, he runs straight home without stopping. He needs to make sure Mamá Coco remembers her father.

When he arrives home, Miguel asks Mamá Coco if she remembers her father. When she can't remember him, Miguel does not give up. He picks up his guitar and plays her father's song. Mamá Coco's face lights up and she starts singing along.

Did You Know?

You can **draw conclusions** using the available facts, or evidence, in the text. How you understand the evidence will help you make a decision about what you have just read.

A Use evidence in the text to answer these questions.

1. Do you think Miguel feels it is important that Mamá Coco remembers her father?

_____

_____

2. What evidence helps you draw your conclusion?

_____

_____

_____

The following year, as always, families prepare their *ofrendas* for *Día de los Muertos*. However, Ernesto de la Cruz's large tomb now looks very different than in previous years. News has spread about how he had poisoned Héctor Rivera. His tomb has a sign on it that says "Forget you."

The Rivera shoe shop also looks different. Tour groups now stop by the shop. The tour guide explains that this was the home of Héctor Rivera, the great songwriter.

B Draw conclusions, using evidence from the text.

1. What conclusion can you draw about Ernesto's reputation? Why do you think so?

_____

_____

_____

2. Do you think Ernesto deserves the reputation he has now? Why or why not?

_____

_____

_____

So, What Did You Think?

Rex, Buzz, and Woody are so excited to be in the science museum! Do you think everyone gets excited about museums?

A Read this text to find out what Sid thinks about museums.

Museum Misery

"Why did I have to come here?" I ask myself as I trudge through the dark rooms. Museums are soooooo boring!

Crushing crowds, dusty dinosaurs, exhausting exhibits—who needs them? Why should we care what happened long ago? I live for now.

As for the interactive displays, I prefer virtual tours, on my own, with my laptop. I don't have to go to boring museums to learn about things.

How about a trip to the zoo instead— where the exhibits are alive?

Hint

Look for statements that are opinions rather than facts.

Did You Know?

Evaluating texts means thinking about what the author seems to want you to think. Decide whether the author's ideas make sense. Do you agree with them?

B Evaluate the text.

1. Summarize the text in one sentence.

_____

2. What is the main idea?

_____

_____

_____

3. Does the author support his ideas with facts? Explain.

_____

_____

_____

4. Do you agree with the author's main idea? Why or why not?

_____

_____

_____

5. What questions do you have after reading the text?

_____

_____

Problem? Solution!

What to Do Next?

Things are changing in the racing world. New, high-tech cars like Jackson Storm are beating older racers like Lightning McQueen.

Pushing himself hard in a race, Lightning suffers a bad crash. He worries about what to do next. One solution is to retire from racing. He has had a great career. Another solution is to practice on equipment that Jackson uses. He could also work with Cruz Ramirez, the best trainer around.

Lightning agrees to train with Cruz. As a result, their hard work pays off for both of them. They are both in terrific racing form!

Did You Know?

In a **problem-and-solution** text structure, the author describes a problem and then presents one or more solutions.

A Complete the problem-and-solution graphic organizer for the story you have just read.

Problem

Hint

Words and phrases such as **problem**, **issue**, **challenge**, **one thing to do**, **another way**, **as a result**, and **the answer is**, are often hints that you are reading a problem-and-solution text.

Solution

Solution

Solution

What Happens

What Makes a Story?

Look at this picture of Randall chasing Mike, Sulley, and Boo. What do you think is the story behind this picture?

As you read this story, think about the **setting**, **characters**, and **plot**.

Saving Boo

Sulley and Mike work at Monsters, Inc., in Monstropolis. Sulley is the top Scarer at Monsters, Inc., and his partner is Mike. They work together to collect energy for Monsters, Inc.

One day, they find Boo, a little girl. Most monsters are terrified of children! But Sulley and Mike decide to help her. They must keep her safe and take her back to her home.

Randall tries to stop them. He makes himself invisible and jumps on Sulley.

Mike comes to the rescue. Sulley gets away, but Randall chases them and tries to take Boo.

When Randall snatches her, Boo fights back. So do Sulley and Mike. They manage to rescue Boo from Randall and carry her away.

Finally, Boo is safe and can go home.

> **Hint**
>
> The setting is usually described at the beginning of the story. Sometimes, you have to make inferences about the setting.

A Use this graphic organizer to outline the story elements for the story you have just read.

Setting

Characters

Plot

Beginning

Middle

End

B Summarize the story in one sentence.

_____

_____

Featuring ... Text Features!

Miguel's favorite instrument is the guitar.

About Guitars

What Guitars Are Made Of

The body of a guitar is made of wood, like maple and walnut. The strings are made of nylon or steel.

How a Guitar Works

Guitars make sound by **vibrating**.

When the player plucks the strings, vibrations travel to the guitar's soundboard. The air inside the body vibrates, too. All the sound then comes out through the sound hole.

Some other parts of a guitar are the

• neck

• bridge

• frets

• tuning pegs

History

Guitars have been used for over 3,000 years. The oldest surviving guitar is from ancient Egypt. Today, guitars are still used around the world to make many types of music.

vibrating: moving back and forth very quickly

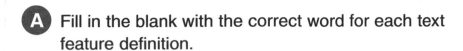

A Fill in the blank with the correct word for each text feature definition.

heading   title   list

paragraph   keyword

Did You Know?

Text features help you know what kind of text you are going to read, like a magazine article or a nonfiction book. Text features help you see how the information is organized.

1. the name of the text

_____

2. a group of sentences that all have to do with the same idea

_____

3. the name of a section of text; it tells what that section is about

_____

4. a word in bold type to show that the text includes a definition for the word, usually in the margin or at the end

_____

5. items set in a text one under the other; often start with a bullet, dash, or number

_____

B Read "About Guitars" again. Underline its text features. Then, label the text features.

Step by Step

Bad Buster! Buster will need a bath after making such a mess.

As you read these **instructions** for giving a dog a bath, think about the text features.

How to Bathe Your Dog

Materials
Tub or sink, towels, washcloth, pitcher or spray bottle, dog shampoo, treats

Steps

1. First, gather your supplies.

2. Place a towel on the bottom of the tub or sink so that your dog won't slip.

3. Place your dog in the tub.

4. Wet your dog's body using the spray bottle or a pitcher. Avoid their face.

5. Use a damp washcloth to gently clean your dog's face. Avoid the ears. They could get infected if they get wet.

6. Apply the shampoo and massage it onto your dog's body.

7. Rinse your dog's body until the water runs clear.

8. Dry your dog with a towel.

9. Finally, give your dog a treat!

Did You Know?

Instructions tell people how to do or make something. They are a list of steps to take, in order. The sentences are usually short. Instructions need to be very clear.

A Draw a (circle) around the correct **purple** word.
Fill in the blanks with an example from the dog
bathing instructions.

1. Instructions are written in the **present** **past** tense.

   Example: _____

   _____

2. Instructions **tell** **ask** readers what to do.

   Example: _____

   _____

3. Instructions are presented in **order** **random order**.

   Example: _____

   _____

4. Instructions may have a list of **materials** **characters**.

   Example: _____

   _____

5. Instructions are very **confusing** **clear**.

   Example: _____

   _____

Seeing Is Believing

Natalie Certain knows the racing statistics of all the racers at the Piston Cup. She can use a table to organize and compare all of her statistics.

A Read the table. Then, answer the questions.

Car Details

Racer	Performance	Body Material
Lightning McQueen	• 0–60 mi in 4 seconds • top speed is 198 mi/h	• cold-rolled sheet metal
Cruz Ramirez	• 0–60 mi in 3.8 seconds • top speed is 210 mi/h	• lightweight alloy
Jackson Storm	• 0–60 mi in 3.6 seconds • top speed is 214 mi/h	• coated carbon fiber and metal composite

1. Who has the fastest top speed?

   _____

2. What material is Lightning's body made of?

   _____

3. How long does it take for Cruz to go from 0 mi to 60 mi?

   _____

4. Explain how you got your answers from the table.

   _____

Did You Know?

Tables have columns (up and down) and rows (across) that are labelled. **Diagrams** are pictures that show how something looks or works. Diagrams have a title and labels. Tables and diagrams let you see details clearly and help you remember the information.

B Examine the diagram of Mack. Answer the questions.

Mack's Parts

smokestack exhaust

rearview mirror

fuel tank

tire

grille

headlight

bumper

1. What does this diagram show?

_____

_____

2. What label could you add to this diagram?

_____

3. What are the lines for in this diagram?

_____

C What other information would you like to see in the diagram?

_____

_____

Let's Talk!

Mike and Sulley pull off an impressive scare at a camp. A reporter from the Monsters University student newspaper, *The Campus Roar*, interviews them.

An Interview with Heroes

Students Mike Wazowski (MW) and James P. Sullivan (JS) pulled off a legendary scare. They tell The Campus Roar (TCR) *what happened.*

TCR: What happened the day of the scare?

MW: I wanted to prove to everyone I was a good Scarer, so I decided to scare a kid by myself.

TCR: Can you tell us about where the scare happened?

MW: I walked through a door into the human world. I first thought I was in a child's bedroom, but it turned out I was in an entire cabin of campers!

TCR: Sulley, how were you feeling knowing that Mike was in the human world by himself?

JS: I was really worried about him.

TCR: What did you do?

JS: I decided to go in after him, even though Dean Hardscrabble told me it was really dangerous.

TCR: What happened when you arrived in the cabin?

JS: The cabin was empty, so I looked for Mike. I found him and we tried to get back, but the door back to Monsters University was locked.

TCR: Mike, how did you feel when you saw the locked door?

MW: We were really worried, but I thought that if we could get enough screams, we could power the door open again.

JS: That is why he is the great Mike Wazowski! We managed to scare all of the camp rangers. They screamed so much, we burst open the door back to Monsters University.

TCR: That's a great ending! Thank you for talking to us today.

A The text features of an interview are listed below. Label "An Interview with Heroes" with these text features.

title   introduction

question   answer

names of people speaking

ending

A True How-To

The marigold is an important flower in Miguel's culture. Many marigolds are planted for *Día de los Muertos*. The marigold's bright color and scent are meant to guide visiting spirits to their *ofrendas* during *Día de los Muerto*s.

Read the instructions on how to plant marigold seeds.

How to Plant Marigold Seeds

Materials
Flowerpot, soil, garden trowel, fertilizer, marigold seeds, water

Steps
1. First, fill the flowerpot three-quarters of the way with soil.

2. Use the garden trowel to turn the soil over and loosen it. Remove any stones.

3. Mix some fertilizer into the soil.

4. Plant the seeds about 6 mm deep and 5 cm apart.

5. Cover them lightly with soil and press gently.

6. Water the seeds.

7. Place the flowerpot in a sunny area. Water every day.

Did You Know?

You can find **instructions** in many places like cookbooks, articles, and even on the back of shampoo bottles.

Hint

Instructions use command statements. Command statements tell people what to do (**Read this book.**).

A Review the instructions on page 76. Write your own instructions for an activity you like.

Title _____

Materials (if any)

_____

_____

Steps

_____

_____

_____

_____

_____

_____

_____

_____

The Moral of the Story

The toys are nervous when Woody tells a scary story. They might prefer a **fable** like "The Cow and the Donkey" instead.

The Cow and the Donkey

One day, Donkey arrived at a farm where Cow was grazing in the field. When Cow saw Donkey come into the field, Cow said, "Go away, Donkey! This is my field, and you are not welcome." Donkey said that she too would be living in the field from now on because she had a job to do.

For a long time, Cow was mean to Donkey. Cow did not show Donkey where to find the best grass to eat. Cow did not talk to Donkey.

Then, one night, Coyote crept into the field and started to sneak toward Cow. But Donkey kicked her strong back legs and cried out loudly, scaring Coyote away. Cow was shaking from fright. "This is the job I was brought here for," said Donkey. "I am here to protect you."

Moral of the story: *Be kind to others!*

Did You Know?

Fables are short pieces of fiction that teach a lesson, or moral. They usually have one to three characters. The characters are usually animals or plants that can talk.

A Use this chart to plan your own fable.

Planning a Fable

Title	
Characters	
Setting	
Problem	
Solution	
Moral	

B Now write your fable. Remember to use the planning chart you created to write your fable.

Hint

Read your fable. Ask yourself
• Have I followed my plan?
• Is there anything missing?
• Is there anything I should change?

What's My Main Idea?

Jackson Storm focuses on one main idea in a race: winning. Writers also focus on one main idea or message when they write.

A Follow these steps to create a main idea.

1. Think of three topic ideas you are interested in writing about. List them below.

_____

_____

_____

_____

2. Choose one topic.

_____

_____

3. Narrow the topic to a main idea.

_____

_____

Did You Know?

To create a **main idea**, ask

- What is the main thing I want to say about this topic?
- What do I want readers to know about this topic?

Write down your main idea to help you stay focused on it while you plan and write. Next steps? Research, and then organize your supporting ideas.

Hint

What does "narrow the topic" mean? It means to make the topic more specific. For example, instead of a story about pirates, a main idea could be a family of pirates who love pancakes.

B List three details that will support your main idea.

1. _____

   _____

2. _____

   _____

3. _____

   _____

C Write a short paragraph about your topic.

_____

_____

_____

_____

_____

_____

_____

Care to Join Us?

Miguel crosses a bridge that joins two worlds.

In language, there are words that act like bridges.
They are called **conjunctions**.

A Complete each sentence with one of these conjunctions: **and**, **but**, or **so**.

1. Dante is hungry, _____ Miguel feeds him.

2. Miguel _____ Mamá Coco enjoy being together.

3. Miguel loves music, _____ Abuelita does not allow him to play it.

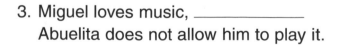

82

B Choose the best conjunction for each sentence.

and   but   so

1. I put on my raincoat _____ dashed to the bus.

2. You look bored, _____ let's play a game.

3. They feel happy _____ excited.

4. I am allergic to peanuts, _____ not to other nuts.

5. My bike tire is flat, _____ I need to fix it.

6. I would love to have a horse, _____ we don't have a barn.

7. She loves both swimming _____ diving.

8. He can't reach the top shelf, _____ he uses a step stool.

Hint

Try each conjunction in each sentence. The right one will show the relationship between the two parts being joined.

C Write a sentence for each conjunction: **and**, **but**, and **so**.

1. _____

2. _____

3. _____

D Write a sentence that uses two conjunctions.

_____

Can-Do Commas

Miguel lives in Santa Cecilia, Mexico. He is excited for *Día de los Muertos*. The celebration begins October 31.

Miguel knows a comma is needed between the names of cities and states and cities and countries. He also knows a comma is needed between the day and the year when writing a date.

A Add a comma where it is needed in the dates and places below.

1. Mexico City Mexico

2. June 6 2020

3. Las Cruces New Mexico

4. September 9 2016

5. Amarillo Texas

6. January 23 2008

7. Puebla Mexico

B Answer the questions making sure to put your commas in the right place.

1. In what city and state/country were you born?

    _____

2. What is your birth date?

    _____

3. In what city and state/country do you live now?

    _____

4. What is a city and state/country you would like to visit?

    _____

5. What is the date of your favorite holiday this year?

    _____

First, Read This

First, Bonnie is scared to go to school. **Next,** Woody sneaks in her backpack to watch over her. **Then,** they both go to school. **Soon,** Bonnie makes Forky. **Finally,** she starts to feel better about school!

A Number the sentences in the order the events take place. The **sequence words** can help you.

_____ Finally, I went to bed, where I would be safe!

_____ Next, I arrived at school, but I tripped on the stairs. Ouch again!

_____ Soon, I recovered and made my way to school.

_____ I managed to get through the rest of the day unharmed.

_____ Then, while eating breakfast, I got grapefruit juice in my eye!

_____ Later that evening, my sister accidentally whacked my thumb.

_____ First, I tripped on my bedroom rug and fell—ouch!

Did You Know?

Sequence words help you put events in the order in which they happen. Some other sequence words are **first**, **then**, **second**, **before**, **after**, **while**, **during**. They don't always have to start the sentence, and they don't have to be used in every sentence.

Hint

Visualize the action and settings to help you put the events in the right order.

B Add sequence words to this paragraph.

first   next   then

soon   later   finally

_____, we unpack the car.

_____, we set up our tent

and stove. _____, we begin

cooking our dinner. _____

we play for a while. _____,

we make a fire. _____, we

head to bed!

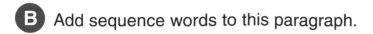
Hint
Some blanks have more than one right answer.

C Write a short paragraph about something you did recently. Use at least four sequence words.

_____

_____

_____

_____

_____

_____

Fuzzy, Fuzzier, Fuzziest

The Oozma Kappa team uses **comparing adjectives** to describe each other: Art is the **fuzziest** member of the team. Sulley is the **tallest**. Don is short, but Mike and Squishy are **shorter**.

You can use comparing adjectives to describe things in your life, too.

A Complete the table by filling in the missing words.

Adjective	Adjective with -er	Adjective with -est
loud		
		saddest
	happier	
funny		
		youngest
	brighter	

Did You Know?

Comparing adjectives are used to compare two or more nouns. To make most comparing adjectives, just add the suffix **-er** or **-est**. For two-syllable adjectives ending in a consonant + **y**, like **fuzzy**, change the **y** to **i** and add the suffix. For words that are a consonant-vowel-consonant, like **big**, double the final consonant (**biggest**).

B Read each sentence. Complete the sentence with the correct form of the **purple** adjective.

1. That was the _____ wind I have ever felt. **strong**

2. My red shirt is _____ than my blue one. **warm**

3. This hike will be _____ than our last one. **tough**

4. The _____ part about visiting Grandpa is saying goodbye. **hard**

5. My cousin tells the _____ jokes you can imagine. **silly**

6. This way is _____ than that way. **quick**

Hint

The adjectives that end in **-est** have **the** in front of them (**the biggest slice**).

C Write a sentence using a comparing adjective of your choice. It can have an **-er** or **-est** ending.

_____

_____

_____

_____

Use Adverbs Happily!

Lightning McQueen tries **anxiously** to get away from Miss Fritter at the Thunder Hollow Speedway demolition derby. Other cars are spinning out **uncontrollably**. Mud flies **everywhere**.

The words **anxiously**, **uncontrollably**, and **everywhere** are **adverbs**.

A Underline the adverb in each sentence. Circle the verb described by the adverb.

1. The demolition derby is held weekly.

2. The cars confidently enter the racetrack.

3. The cars drive quickly.

4. All the engines roar noisily.

5. The cars navigate around obstacles.

6. Cars frequently crash into the obstacles.

7. Cruz Ramirez bravely enters the race.

8. New racers are sometimes welcomed rudely.

9. Cruz happily finishes in first place.

10. The crowd cheers wildly!

Did You Know?

An **adverb** is a word that describes a verb. It tells how, where, or when an action is done. Many adverbs are adjectives with the ending **-ly** added, (**safe** – **safely**, **kind** – **kindly**).

Hint

An adverb can go before or after the verb, but it stays close to the verb, without many other words between.

B Turn each **purple** word into an adverb.

1. I eat my ice cream _____. **slow**

2. He trudges _____. **tired**

3. They _____ lift the heavy box. **awkward**

4. The wolf licked its lips _____. **hungry**

5. _____, I add an egg to the batter. **careful**

6. I email my grandparents _____. **month**

7. She _____ held the door for everyone. **thoughtful**

8. The town _____ planted trees at the dog park. **wise**

C Write two sentences that use adverbs.
<u>Underline</u> the verbs described by the adverbs.

1. _____

_____

2. _____

_____

Who Owns What?

Miguel shares **his** secret with Dante. The secret is **theirs**.

Without **possessive adjectives** and **pronouns**, we would not know who the secret belonged to.

A Draw a (circle) around the correct **possessive adjective** in each sentence.

1. I am proud of   my   me   effort this year.

2. All the birds have flown from   its   their   nests.

3. We should practice   our   her   presentation.

4. Ellie forgot   me   her   lunch again.

5. The cat cleans   its   their   whiskers.

6. You and Amar can clean up   you   your toys now.

Did You Know?

A **possessive adjective** (**my, your, her, his, its, our, their**) describes the noun that follows it. It shows who or what the noun belongs to.
A **possessive pronoun** (**mine, yours, his, hers, ours, yours, theirs**) takes the place of a noun.

B Write a sentence for each of the possessive adjectives.

our   your   their

1. _____

2. _____

3. _____

C Fill in the blank with the correct possessive pronoun.

mine   his   hers   ours   yours   theirs

1. Ernesto de la Cruz got many gifts from his fans.

   The gifts are _____.

2. The Los Chachalacos band has a sousaphone.

   The sousaphone is _____.

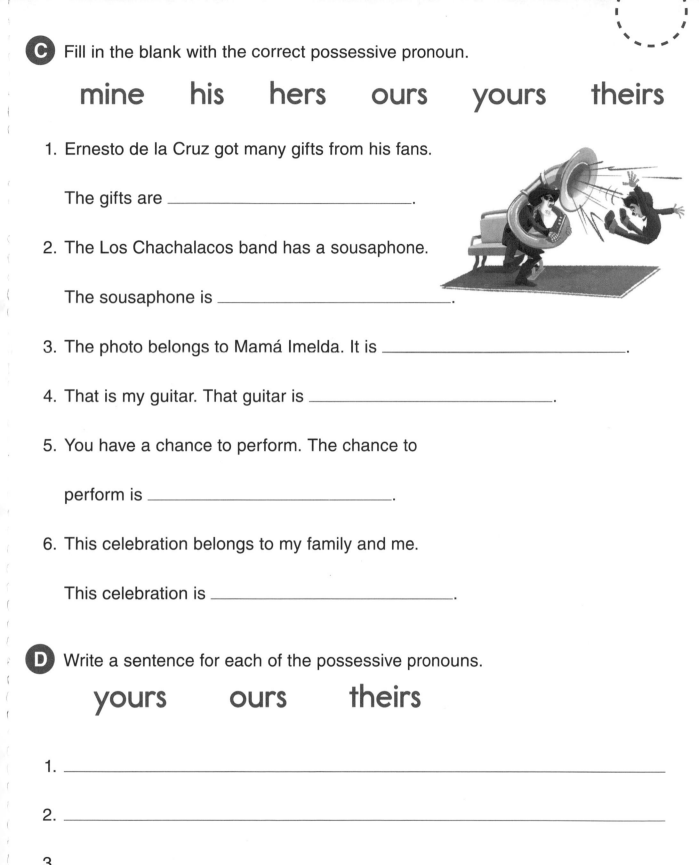

3. The photo belongs to Mamá Imelda. It is _____.

4. That is my guitar. That guitar is _____.

5. You have a chance to perform. The chance to

   perform is _____.

6. This celebration belongs to my family and me.

   This celebration is _____.

D Write a sentence for each of the possessive pronouns.

yours   ours   theirs

1. _____

2. _____

3. _____

Plural Practice

Cruz Ramirez has training strategies she uses to get racers into shape.

There are also strategies for making nouns plural.

Some just need an added **s**.

car → cars

If a noun ends in **sh**, **ch**, **s**, or **x**, add **es**.

crash → crashes

If a noun ends with a consonant and a **y**, drop the **y** and add **ies**.

trophy → trophies

Some irregular words don't follow these patterns.

child → children

A Circle the correct plural noun for each word.

fox	cherry	dish
foxs	cherries	dishs
foxes	cherrys	dishes

couch	book	bus
couches	bookes	busies
couchs	books	buses

B Circle the correct plural noun for each word.

calf	man	mouse
calves	mens	moose
calvs	men	mice

person	foot	woman
people	feets	women
persons	feet	womans

Being Proper

The city of **Monstropolis** has a company called **Monsters, Inc.** Some monsters work there as **Scarers**.

The **purple** words above are **proper nouns**. Can you think of some other proper nouns?

A Underline each proper noun in these sentences.

1. Our neighbor, Mrs. Kovac, sometimes bakes

   for us.

2. One day I hope to visit Cavendish Beach.

3. We usually buy our vegetables at Fresh

   Country Market.

4. My oldest cousin is moving to Australia.

5. Scooter is the name of my friend's gerbil.

6. My favorite month is May.

B Correct the capitalization error(s) in each sentence.

1. We go to the dentist's office on tuesday.

_____

2. My teacher's favorite Country is Iceland.

_____

3. I belong to a club called ms. harvie's Dance World.

_____

4. My younger Sister loves hockey.

_____

5. The title of my book is *danger marshmallows*.

_____

C Answer each question with a proper noun.

1. Where do you live? _____

2. What is your full name? _____

3. What country would you like to visit? _____

4. What is a restaurant near you? _____

5. What is your favorite book or movie? _____

Abstract Activities

Mike felt great **pride** in his job at Monsters, Inc.

Pride is an **abstract noun**. Abstract nouns name feelings, concepts, and ideas. Some examples are **childhood**, **wisdom**, and **hope**.

A Underline the abstract noun or nouns in each sentence.

1. Sulley forms a friendship with Boo.

2. Sulley brings Boo great joy.

3. The citizens of Monstropolis feel fear when they see children.

4. Waternoose did not tell the truth.

5. Mike and Sulley rid Monstropolis of the prejudice against children.

6. They found that laughter could power Monstropolis.

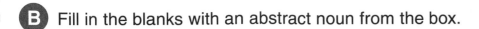

B Fill in the blanks with an abstract noun from the box.

knowledge   courage   dream   hope

1. Mike's childhood _____ was to be
   a Scarer.

2. Mike has a lot of _____ about working at
   Monsters, Inc.

3. Sulley shows _____ when he decides to
   help Boo.

4. Mike and Sulley have _____ that they can
   make children laugh.

C Write three sentences of your own that use abstract nouns. Use the nouns
from the exercises or think of your own.

1. _____

2. _____

3. _____

Making Sense of Tense

Ducky and Bunny **play** today. They **played** yesterday, too.

A Underline the **verb** in each sentence. Check the correct **verb tense**: **past** or **present**.

1. I help my dad with chores.

    _____ past   _____ present

2. Our bus stops at the railway crossing.

    _____ past   _____ present

3. We planted cucumbers in the spring.

    _____ past   _____ present

4. The seagulls screeched overhead.

    _____ past   _____ present

5. We race toward the swings.

    _____ past   _____ present

6. I watched the sunset last night.

    _____ past   _____ present

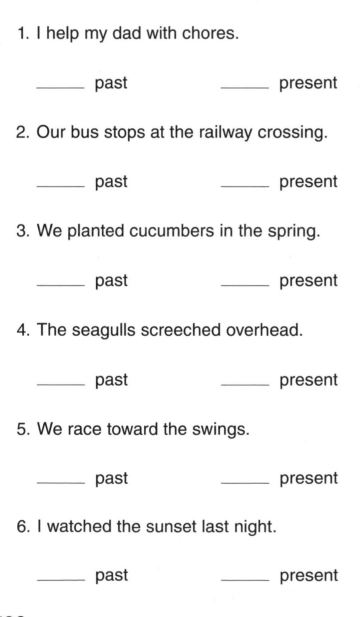

Did You Know?

Verbs in the **present tense** describe an action that is happening right now. (I **play** soccer.) The **past tense** of a verb describes an action that has happened before. (I **played** soccer.) How did the verb **play** change when it became past tense? Not all past tense verbs use an **-ed** ending. Some verbs are irregular (the verb **buy** becomes **bought**; the verb **to be** becomes **was** or **were**).

B Write the past tense for these irregular verbs.

1. throw _____

2. run _____

3. say _____

4. eat _____

5. see _____

6. do _____

C Change each **purple** verb to the past tense.

1. I _____ an email to my friend
   last night. **type**

2. They _____ to shut the gate
   again. **forget**

3. The kite _____ well yesterday.
   flies

4. She _____ the winning goal.
   scores

5. We _____ cupcakes for
   yesterday's bake sale. **make**

6. He _____ down on the bed
   with his blanket. **lie**

> **Hint**
>
> For past-tense verbs
> ending in silent **e**, just
> add **d** (**rake** becomes
> **raked**).

Ready, Set, Action!

When Chick Hicks describes races, he uses a lot of precise **action verbs**. Instead of using the verb **drive**, he likes to say **zoom**, **explode**, **fly**, **surge**, or **blaze** instead. Action verbs help his descriptions sound more exciting!

A Change each **purple** verb to a more precise action verb. Cross out the first verb. The first one is done for you.

1. I ~~walk~~ **stroll** to the park.

2. We **speak** _____ with the store manager.

3. She **laughs** _____ at the comedian's joke.

4. He **sees** _____ an eagle in the tree.

5. I **take** _____ the heavy box to the truck.

6. We **eat** _____ the delicious pizza.

7. He **says** _____ "Hey!" when he sees the bear.

8. I **ran** _____ home.

Did You Know?

Action verbs describe things that can be done. They also describe feelings and thoughts (**enjoy**, **assume**, **think**). Choosing **precise action verbs** helps your readers visualize exactly what you mean.

Hint

Use a thesaurus to help you expand your vocabulary and choose more precise action verbs.

B Solve each clue. Add the missing letters to complete the precise action verb.

1. to look very closely at something   e____a____ine

2. to run like a horse   g____l____o____

3. to speak very softly   ____h____s____er

4. to shut a door loudly   ____ ____am

5. to drink something noisily   s____ur____

C Write a description of something exciting you have done or seen. Use precise action verbs.

_____

_____

_____

_____

_____

_____

_____

_____

Quality Control

These employees at Monsters, Inc. check closely to catch any mistakes at the factory.

Writers need to check their work, too. After you have planned, written, and revised something, the next step is to edit it.

A Each sentence has three mistakes. Edit the sentences.

1. our vacation was a dreamm—except for for

   the mosquitoes!

2. She asKed, "Where is the noyse coming from"

3. Excietment was in the air at nunavut's

   biggest park..

4. In october, I can sea the leaves change Color.

5. the firefihgters flew into action!.

6. With four left seconds, Natasha shoots—and

   theball swishes in the hoop

7. Hurricane harvey brought hevy rain and

   strong w inds.

8. Their aren't many of you're paintings left.?

B An editing checklist can help you edit.
Complete this checklist.

Editing Checklist

☐ Are words spelled

_____?

☐ Does each sentence _____
with an uppercase letter?

☐ Does each sentence end with a

period, _____, or
exclamation mark?

☐ Are sequence words in the right

_____?

☐ Are verbs in the correct

_____?

☐ Are _____ nouns
capitalized?

Taking Numbers Apart

Hundreds of marigold petals swirl around Miguel as he plays Ernesto de la Cruz's guitar.

A Fill in the blanks to complete the expanded form of each number.

1. 745 ___7___ hundreds + ___4___ tens + ___5___ ones

2. 220 ___2___ hundreds + ___2___ tens + ___0___ ones

3. 108 ___1___ hundreds + ___0___ tens + ___8___ ones

4. 576 ___5___ hundreds + ___7___ tens + ___6___ ones

5. 621 ___6___ hundreds + ___2___ tens + ___1___ ones

6. 79 ___0___ hundreds + ___7___ tens + ___9___ ones

> **Did You Know?**
>
> Numbers can be written out in three ways: standard form (423), words (four hundred twenty-three), and expanded form (4 hundreds + 2 tens + 3 ones or 400 + 20 + 3).

B Write these numbers in words.

1. 739 ___Seven hundred 39___

2. 804 ___eight hundred Four___

3. 520 ___Five hundred Twenty___

4. 213 ___Two hundred Thirteen___

5. 107 ___One hundred seven___

C Complete the table.

Standard Form	Words	Expanded Form
462	four hundred sixty-two	400 + 60 + 2
696	SIX huNdred	600 + 90 + 6
91	NINTY one	90 + 1
348	Three huNded	300 + 40 + 8
952	NiNehuNdred	900 + 50 + 2
736	Seve N hunda	700 + 30 + 6
501	Five hundred	500 + 1
17	seventeen	10 + 7
893	eight hundred ninety-three	800 + 90 + 3
48	forty-eight	40 + 8
111	ONe huNdred	100 + 10 + 1
288	two hundred eighty-eight	200 + 80 + 8
104	oNe huNdred FOUR	100 + 4

Get in Position!

Chick Hicks likes collecting race stickers. He is covered in 318 stickers!

Base ten blocks can be used to represent numbers. 318 is represented by 3 flats, 1 rod, and 8 units.

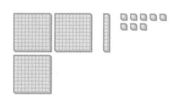

A Match the numbers with the correct base ten block descriptions.

<table>
<tr><td>1. 50</td><td>3 flats, 7 rods, 9 units</td></tr>
<tr><td>2. 184</td><td>5 rods</td></tr>
<tr><td>3. 611</td><td>8 flats, 0 rods, 8 units</td></tr>
<tr><td>4. 379</td><td>1 flat, 8 rods, 4 units</td></tr>
<tr><td>5. 808</td><td>6 flats, 1 rod, 1 unit</td></tr>
<tr><td>6. 13</td><td>9 flats, 3 rods, 3 units</td></tr>
<tr><td>7. 93</td><td>1 rod, 3 units</td></tr>
<tr><td>8. 933</td><td>9 rods, 3 units</td></tr>
</table>

Did You Know?

Base ten blocks can help you understand the place value of numbers. Hundreds are represented by flats. Tens are represented by rods. Ones are represented by units.

B Draw base ten blocks to model each of the numbers. The first one is done for you.

Number	Hundreds	Tens	Ones
225	▢ ▢	‖	▫ ▫ ▫ ▫ ▫
95			
432			

C Choose one of the above numbers and model the number a different way using base ten blocks.

Number	Hundreds	Tens	Ones

Hint

Think of regrouping 1 rod as 10 unit blocks or 1 flat as 10 rods.

I'm the Greatest!

Jackson Storm beats Lightning McQueen because Jackson's speed is faster, or greater.

 A <u>Underline</u> the greatest number in each row. Draw the base ten blocks to model the greatest number.

1. 31   101   41

Hundreds	Tens	Ones

Hint

When you are comparing two numbers, remember that a two-digit number has no hundreds. A three-digit number will have at least one hundred, so it will be greater than a two-digit number.

2. 92   259   251

Hundreds	Tens	Ones

3. 444   445   450

Hundreds	Tens	Ones

B Draw a (circle) around the greatest number in each set.

1. ninety	one hundred one	one hundred ten
2. nine hundred nine	nine hundred ten	nine hundred eight
3. 7 hundreds + 7 tens + 7 ones	7 hundreds + 1 ten + 7 ones	7 hundreds + 0 tens + 7 ones
4. five hundred forty-two	four hundred twenty-nine	six hundred seventy-three
5. 5 hundreds + 2 tens + 1 one	5 hundreds + 0 tens + 1 one	5 hundreds + 1 ten + 1 one

C Which car has the greatest average speed?
Rank the cars from fastest to slowest.

Car	Average Speed	Ranking
Cruz Ramirez	2 hundreds + 7 ones mi/h	
Jackson Storm	2 hundreds + 9 ones mi/h	
Lightning McQueen	1 hundred + 8 tens + 15 ones mi/h	
Chase Racelott	2 hundreds + 4 ones mi/h	

Hint

Sometimes, tens can be represented by ones. For example, 64 can be represented by 6 tens and 4 ones. It can also be represented as 5 tens and 14 ones.

Smallest and Largest

As Miguel walks through the Land of the Dead, he sees many buildings. Some buildings in the Land of the Dead have many homes. Some buildings have just a few.

A Each number represents the amount of homes in a building. In each row, draw a (circle) around the smallest number. <u>Underline</u> the largest number.

1. 24	702	554	87
2. 330	530	942	120
3. 98	101	102	105
4. 202	208	210	201
5. 657	756	675	765
6. 994	94	904	949

Did You Know?

When one number is smaller than another, we can show this using a **less than** sign (2 < 5). To show that one number is larger than another, we can use the **more than** sign (9 > 7).

B Write < or > to make each number statement true.

1. 101 _____ 98

2. 592 _____ 590

3. 608 _____ 680

4. 875 _____ 857

5. 253 _____ 235

C Write < or > to make each number statement true.
Explain how you know.

1. 303 _____ 503

_____

_____

2. 422 _____ 402

_____

_____

3. 750 _____ 650

_____

_____

D Determine which number statements are not true.
Rewrite them correctly.

1. 555 < 505 _____

2. 98 < 105 _____

3. 471 < 417 _____

4. 17 > 117 _____

What's the Order?

Sulley and Mike have scare practice every
night. Their scaring is getting really good!

A Organize the number of times they scare
from least to greatest.

1. 385   212   198   387   306

_____

2. 785   796   801   800   797

_____

3. 164   99   97   500   275

_____

Hint

Working from left to
right can help you
order numbers. Start by
comparing the hundreds
value. Then, compare
the tens value, and then
compare the ones value.

4. 751   75   750   570   57

_____

5. 66   6   660   606   661

_____

6. 991   499   389   950   999

_____

B Which numbers can you make using the digits **1 5 3**?

1. Make the largest number possible. _____

2. Make the smallest number possible. _____

3. Write four more numbers that you can make using the digits **1 5 3**.

_____ _____ _____ _____

4. Order all the numbers that you made from least to greatest.

_____, _____, _____, _____, _____, _____

C Sulley and Mike count the number of scare cans in the door tech lab every day for one week.

590   293   887   878   367   356   778

1. Write the numbers in order from least to greatest.

_____

_____

2. Explain how you knew in which order to put the numbers.

_____

_____

Rounding the Curve

Cruz Ramirez wears number 51. You can round her number to the nearest ten, which is 50.

A Use the number line to help you round to the nearest ten as you answer each question.

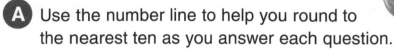

1. Find 61 on the number line. Which tens value is it closer to, 60 or 70?

_____

2. Find 86 on the number line. Which tens value is it closer to, 80 or 90?

_____

Did You Know?

Numbers that end in 5 to 9 are rounded up to the nearest ten. Numbers that end in 1 to 4 are rounded down to the nearest ten.

B Round each number to the nearest ten.

1. 18 _____   2. 86 _____

3. 33 _____   4. 5 _____

5. 57 _____   6. 60 _____

7. 74 _____   8. 49 _____

9. 22 _____   10. 91 _____

C Round each car's number to the nearest ten.

Car	Car Number	Nearest Ten
	94	
	11	
	19	
	58	

D Round these numbers to the nearest ten.

1. 25 _____

2. 188 _____

3. 177 _____

4. 834 _____

5. 350 _____

6. 856 _____

7. 215 _____

8. 567 _____

9. 463 _____

10. 999 _____

Hint

When rounding three-digit numbers to the nearest ten, focus on the tens and ones. If you have a three-digit number that ends in 95 through 99, it will round up to the next hundred (297 rounds up to 300).

Evenly Split

Mike really likes pizza! His favorite pizza has mushrooms, pepperoni, and eyeballs on it. He eats a slice of pizza with mushrooms and eyeballs.

A Mike took his slice from the pizza below. Answer questions about the pizza by writing fractions out in words.

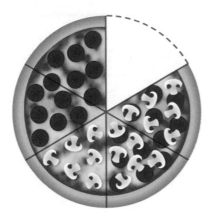

Did You Know?

A fraction includes a **numerator** and a **denominator**. In a fraction, the parts are always of equal size.

1. What fraction of the pizza did Mike take? _____

2. What fraction of the pizza is left over? _____

3. What fraction of the pizza has pepperoni? _____

4. What fraction of the pizza has mushrooms? _____

5. What fraction of the pizza has eyeballs? _____

6. What fraction of the pizza has pepperoni and mushrooms? _____

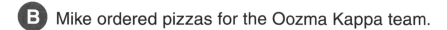

B Mike ordered pizzas for the Oozma Kappa team.

1. Draw mushrooms on two thirds of this pizza.

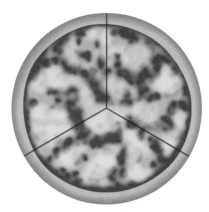

2. If Mike eats one slice of this pizza, what fraction is left? Write out the fraction using words.

_____

3. Draw pepperoni slices on four quarters of this pizza.

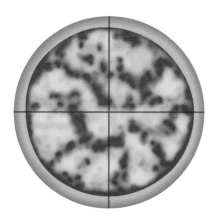

4. If Mike wants the biggest slice of pizza, should he choose a slice of mushroom pizza or pepperoni pizza? How do you know?

_____

_____

Fearless Fractions

Skulls are an important symbol of *Día de los Muertos*, or Day of the Dead. The skulls represent the people who are being remembered. There are many skulls on the Rivera family's altar.

A Use words to write fractions for the set of skulls.

1. What fraction of skulls have closed mouths?

   _____

2. What fraction of skulls have candles in their eyes?

   _____

3. What fraction of skulls are showing teeth?

   _____

4. What fraction of skulls have two eyes?

   _____

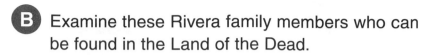

B Examine these Rivera family members who can be found in the Land of the Dead.

1. What fraction of family members shown wear earrings?

_____

2. What fraction of family members shown are women?

_____

3. What fraction of family members shown are men?

_____

4. What fraction of family members shown can be found in the Land of the Dead?

_____

Let's Share

Bonnie got a lollipop from the carnival. She wants $\frac{2}{8}$ of the lollipop. She wants to share $\frac{1}{4}$ of the lollipop.

$\frac{2}{8}$

$\frac{1}{4}$

The fractions of lollipop are the same! These fractions are **equivalent** or the same.

A Compare the fractions. Use >, <, or =.

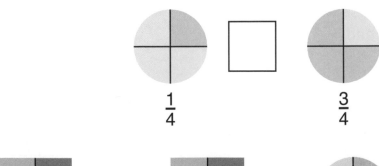

$\frac{1}{4}$ $\frac{3}{4}$

$\frac{1}{2}$ $\frac{2}{4}$ $\frac{1}{3}$ $\frac{5}{8}$

B Write the fraction for each figure. Then, compare
using <, >, or =.

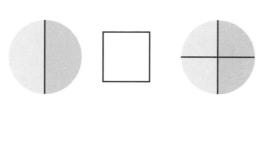

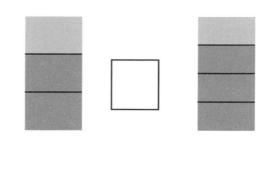

_____ _____

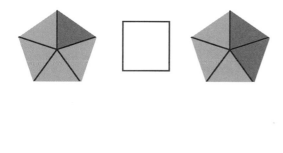

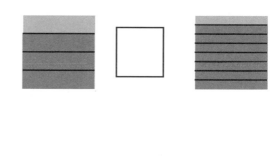

_____ _____

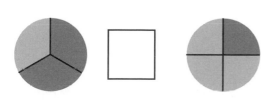

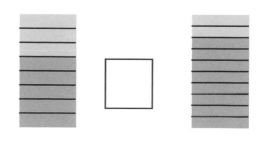

_____ _____

Take Note

Miguel loves music. He enjoys singing and playing the guitar. Music has notes that are described as fractions, such as $\frac{1}{2}$ notes or $\frac{1}{4}$ notes. Which note do you think is held for longer? Think about which one is bigger.

Did You Know?

$\frac{1}{2}$, $\frac{1}{4}$, and $\frac{1}{8}$ are musical note values. 1 is also a musical note value. It is called a whole note.

A Write the fractions on the number line.

$$\frac{3}{8} \qquad \frac{1}{2} \qquad \frac{1}{8}$$

$$\frac{1}{4} \qquad \frac{7}{8} \qquad \frac{5}{8} \qquad \frac{3}{4}$$

0 ————————————————— 1

B Represent both fractions by shading the fraction strip. Circle the greater fraction.

1. $\frac{4}{5}$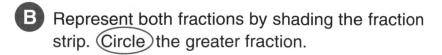

   $\frac{2}{3}$

2. $\frac{2}{4}$

   $\frac{3}{5}$

3. $\frac{1}{3}$

   $\frac{1}{4}$

4. $\frac{3}{5}$

   $\frac{3}{4}$

5. How did you determine which fraction is greater?

_____

_____

Money, Money, Money

Hamm is collecting money for Bonnie to spend at the carnival.

A Use words to write each amount. The first one is done for you.

1. $1.75   **one dollar and seventy-five cents**

2. $2.50 _____

_____

3. $2.80 _____

_____

4. $3.15 _____

_____

5. $5.35 _____

_____

6. $7.90 _____

_____

> ### Did You Know?
>
> In the United States, money amounts are written using a dollar sign ($). The dollar sign is placed to the left of the amount ($7.62). If an amount is less than a dollar, you can still use the dollar sign. For example, **thirty-five cents** can be written as **35¢** or **$0.35**.

B Write the value for each group of coins and bills.

1.

_____

2.

_____

3.

_____

4.

_____

5.

_____

6.

_____

Counting Ahead

Mike is ready to start studying! He borrows 10 books from the library each day.

A Use the chart to answer the following questions.

Write in the missing numbers on the chart.

10	20	30	40	50	60	70	80	90	100
	120	130	140	150	160	170	180	190	200
210	220		240	250	260	270	280		
310	320	330		350	360	370	380	390	400
410				450	460	470	480	490	500
510	520	530	540	550	560			590	600
610	620	630	640		660		680		700
710	720	730	740	750	760	770	780	790	800
910		930	940	950		970	980	990	

B Use the completed chart to help you skip count.

1. Start at 210 and count forward by 10s to 300.

_____

2. Start at 850 and count forward by 10s to 1000.

_____

C Mike has a big test coming up. He borrows 25 books each day. Use the number lines to practice counting forward by 25s.

1. If Mike borrows 25 books every day for eight days, how many books does he have? _____

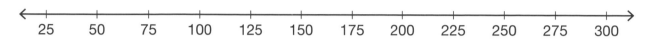

2. Start at 300 and count forward by 25s to 575. Write the numbers you counted.

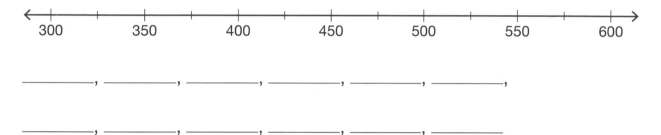

_____ , _____ , _____ , _____ , _____ , _____ ,

_____ , _____ , _____ , _____ , _____ , _____

3. Start at 675 and count forward by 25s to 1000. Write the numbers you counted.

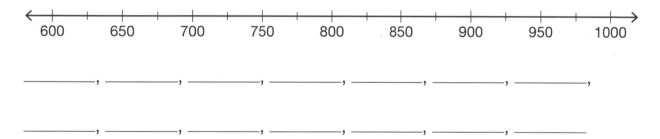

_____ , _____ , _____ , _____ , _____ , _____ , _____ ,

_____ , _____ , _____ , _____ , _____ , _____ , _____

4. Extend this pattern after 1000 for two more numbers. What are those numbers? _____ , _____

Skip to It!

It's time to clean up the track after Lightning McQueen's race. There are 100 tires to put away. The tires are in stacks of 10.

A Use a number line to count how many stacks need to be put away. Start at 100 and skip count backward by 10s.

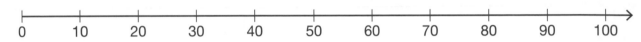

Number of tire stacks that need to be put away: _____

B Use the number line to skip count backward.

1. Count backward by 10s starting at 95 and ending at 65.

   _____ , _____ , _____ , _____

2. Count backward by 10s starting at 77 and ending at 57.

   _____ , _____ , _____

> ### Did You Know?
> Skip counting is not just a helpful way to count numbers faster. It also helps you to see patterns.

3. Count backward by 10s starting at 82 and ending at 52.

   _____ , _____ , _____ , _____

4. Count backward by 10s starting at 99 and ending at 59.

   _____ , _____ , _____ , _____

C Tickets to Lightning's next race, the Florida 500, are selling quickly. Use the number line to skip count backward by 5s.

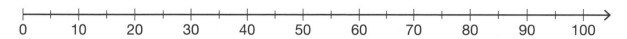

0 10 20 30 40 50 60 70 80 90 100

1. Count backward by 5s starting from 100 and ending at 50.

————, ————, ————, ————, ————, ————,

————, ————, ————, ————, ————

2. Count backward by 5s starting at 75 and ending at 45.

————, ————, ————, ————, ————, ————, ————

3. Count backward by 5s starting at 54 and ending at 24.

————, ————, ————, ————, ————, ————, ————

4. Count backward by 5s starting at 43 and ending at 13.

————, ————, ————, ————, ————, ————, ————

D Complete the number patterns.

1. 368, 358, ————, ————, ————, ————, 308

2. 900, 800, ————, ————, ————, ————, 300

3. 586, 581, ————, ————, ————, ————, 556

Write On!

Every race car needs a number, even the ones at the Crazy Eight demolition derby. One of the derby stars is Miss Fritter. She uses the number **58**. This number can be written out in words as **fifty-eight**.

A Review number words by writing the race car numbers using words.

1. 71 _____

2. 88 _____

3. 97 _____

4. 29 _____

5. 13 _____

6. 12 _____

7. 33 _____

8. 0 _____

Did You Know?

As in all spelling, there are some exceptions to the way numbers are written. For example, the number 4 is spelled **four**, but the number 40 is spelled **forty**, without the **u**.

B Many fans watch the Crazy Eight demolition derby. Write out the number of fans in words.

1. 561 _____

2. 244 _____

3. 746 _____

4. 913 _____

5. 188 _____

6. 399 _____

7. 608 _____

Hint

To write three-digit numbers in words, start with the hundreds, then the tens, and finally the ones.

C Complete the number patterns below.

1. six hundred, _____,

_____, three hundred, two hundred

2. two, twelve, _____,

_____, _____,

fifty-two

3. three hundred forty-seven, _____,

_____, _____,

three hundred seven

Sheepish Sums

Bo Peep has lost her sheep. The Aliens want to help Bo Peep. They add cotton balls to their bodies to pretend to be sheep.

A Write out all the possible pairs of numbers for each sum.

1. sum of 10

2. sum of 8

3. sum of 5

B Calculate these sums using mental math.

1. 9 + 9 = _____

2. 12 + 6 = _____

3. 50 + 20 = _____

4. 25 + 25 = _____

5. 41 + 41 = _____

6. 13 + 87 = _____

7. 65 + 18 = _____

8. 16 + 61 = _____

9. 22 + 13 = _____

10. 59 + 15 = _____

> **Hint**
>
> Use the first number to make a number pair that adds to 10 with the second number. Then, complete the sum. For example, 5 + 6 = ?
> **6** can be expressed as **5 + 1**.
> **5 + 5 = 10**
> **10 + 1 = 11**
> **5 + 6 = 11**

C The Aliens find more cotton balls in the bathroom. They already have 18 cotton balls. If they add 6 more cotton balls, how many cotton balls do they have in total?

Use mental math to calculate the sum.
Explain your answer.

_____

_____

_____

What's Left?

Bonnie wants to win some prizes at the carnival! She has 21 tickets and wants to turn some in for prizes.

A Use mental math strategies to help Bonnie. Explain how you got each answer.

1. How many tickets will be left if she spends 12 on a teddy bear?

   21 − 12 = _____

   _____

   _____

   _____

   _____

> **Hint**
>
> The **friendly number strategy** is a mental math strategy.
> Example:
> **34 − 23 = ?**
> 23 is **10 + 10 + 3**
> Subtract 10 from 34
> **34 − 10 = 24**
> Subtract 10 from 24
> **24 − 10 = 14**
> Subtract 3 from 14
> **14 − 3 = 11**
> So, 34 − 23 = **11**

2. How many tickets will be left If she spends 17 on a toy frog?

   21 − 17 = _____

   _____

   _____

   _____

   _____

B Subtract using a mental math strategy.

1. 42 − 22 = _____   2. 19 − 12 = _____

3. 34 − 14 = _____   4. 66 − 33 = _____

5. 28 − 17 = _____   6. 44 − 23 = _____

7. 38 − 21 = _____   8. 79 − 56 = _____

9. 53 − 25 = _____   10. 50 − 25 = _____

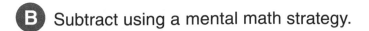

Hint

The **adding up strategy** is a mental math strategy.
Example:
34 − 23 = ?
You want to add up from 23 until you reach 34.
Add **7** to 23 to reach 30
23 + 7 = 30
Add **4** to 30 to reach 34
30 + 4 = 34
7 + 4 = 11
So, 34 − 23 = **11**

C Now, Bonnie has 56 tickets she wants to spend.
If she spends 14, how many does she have left?
Use a mental math strategy to solve the problem.
Explain how you got your answer.

_____

_____

_____

What's the Total?

Miguel's town is preparing for *Día de los Muertos* by hanging paper banners called *papel picado* from houses. Each street is decorated with many banners.

A Use regrouping to calculate the number of papel picado hanging along different streets. Show your work by drawing base ten blocks for each question.

1. 347 + 125 = _____

Hundreds	Tens	Ones

2. 132 + 228 = _____

Hundreds	Tens	Ones

B Calculate each sum.

1.
$$316 \\ + 422$$

2.
$$334 \\ + 353$$

3.
$$553 \\ + 116$$

4.
$$161 \\ + 125$$

5.
$$722 \\ + 250$$

6.
$$274 \\ + 210$$

7.
$$255 \\ + 236$$

8.
$$326 \\ + 227$$

9.
$$445 \\ + 149$$

C Miguel's town only has space to hang 800 papel picado. The townspeople hang 485 papel picado one night. They still have 287 more papel picado to hang. Is there enough space for these papel picado? Calculate and explain your answer.

Hint

When you are adding numbers, you may need to regroup them. For example, 37 is 2 tens and 17 ones or 3 tens and 7 ones.

_____

_____

_____

_____

Driving Differences

Lightning McQueen wants to train on Fireball Beach. Cruz Ramirez follows him there, but she keeps getting stuck in the sand.

A Lightning reaches a top speed of 197 mi/h at Fireball Beach, while Cruz reaches 189 mi/h. What is the difference between their top speeds on the beach?

$$\begin{array}{r} 197 \\ -\ 189 \\ \hline \end{array}$$

Did You Know?

Words like **difference**, **decrease**, **fewer**, and **how many more** all tell you to subtract.

B Calculate each difference.

1. $\begin{array}{r} 734 \\ -\ 432 \\ \hline \end{array}$

2. $\begin{array}{r} 889 \\ -\ 679 \\ \hline \end{array}$

3. $\begin{array}{r} 509 \\ -\ 105 \\ \hline \end{array}$

4. $\begin{array}{r} 462 \\ -\ 341 \\ \hline \end{array}$

5. $\begin{array}{r} 178 \\ -\ 126 \\ \hline \end{array}$

6. $\begin{array}{r} 377 \\ -\ 270 \\ \hline \end{array}$

7.
651
− 417

8.
563
− 259

9.
182
− 175

10.
271
− 253

11.
534
− 426

12.
494
− 177

13.
776
− 558

14.
338
− 129

15.
980
− 351

C Solve each word problem.

1. Cruz completes 290 practice laps in one week. Lightning completes 350 practice laps in one week. How many more practice laps does Lightning complete than Cruz?

2. The following week, Lightning completes 70 fewer practice laps and Cruz completes 50 more than each did the week before. How many more laps does Cruz complete than Lightning?

Working Together

The Green Army Men line up in three pairs to carry a baby monitor downstairs. Three pairs can be expressed as **2 + 2 + 2** or **3 × 2**.

A Use the number lines to help you skip count, add, and multiply.

1. Show 2 + 2 + 2 on the number line.

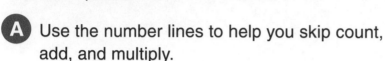

Write the addition sentence.

_____

Write the **multiplication fact**.

_____

2. Show 3 + 3 + 3 on the number line.

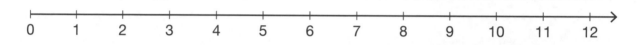

Write the addition sentence.

_____

Write the multiplication fact.

_____

B Fill in the blanks with the correct factors. Calculate each product. You can use the number line to help you.

```
|++++|++++|++++|++++|++++|++++|++++|++++|++++|++++|→
0         10         20         30         40         50
```

1. _____ × 2 = 12   2. 2 × 8 = _____

3. 3 × 7 = _____   4. 4 × 6 = _____

Hint

Start at 0 when using a number line to show repeated addition.

5. 4 × 5 = _____   6. 6 × _____ = 42

7. 5 × 6 = _____   8. 5 × 3 = _____

9. 7 × _____ = 28   10. 7 × 7 = _____

C Draw a picture to represent each set of words. Write a multiplication fact for each set.

1. 6 groups of 3 Aliens

_____

2. 4 groups of 4 Aliens

_____

Set It Up!

It is time to set up traffic cones at the Florida International Super Speedway.

A There are 21 traffic cones that need to be divided into sets of 3.

1. Circle the traffic cones in sets of 3.

2. How many sets are there? _____

3. Write the division sentence. _____

B There are 16 traffic cones that need to be divided into sets of 4.

1. Circle the traffic cones in sets of 4.

2. How many sets are there? _____

3. Write the division sentence. _____

> **Did You Know?**
>
> In the equation $20 \div 5 = 4$, 20 is the **dividend**, 5 is the **divisor**, and 4 is the **quotient**.

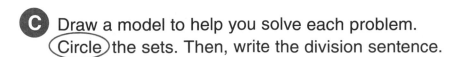

C Draw a model to help you solve each problem. Circle the sets. Then, write the division sentence.

1. 20 traffic cones divided into 5 sets

> **Hint**
>
> Draw the total number of items first. Then, draw a circle around each set. Continue until all the items are circled.

_____

2. 24 tires divided into 4 sets

_____

D Cruz Ramirez and Lightning McQueen knock over 18 cones during a practice race.

1. If they both hit an equal number of cones, how many cones do they each hit? Write the division sentence.

_____

2. Label the dividend, divisor, and quotient.

More and More

Mike and Sulley take scaring very seriously. They want to be the best scaring team at Monsters University!

A Mike and Sulley sign out a lot of books on scaring from the library. Write two multiplication sentences for this **array** of library books.

Did You Know?

An array can help you solve a multiplication or division sentence.

_____

_____

B Write two multiplication sentences for each array.

1.

2.

_____

_____

_____

_____

C Solve each multiplication fact. Sketch an array for each multiplication fact.

1. $2 \times 6 =$ _____

2. $3 \times 3 =$ _____

3. $4 \times 4 =$ _____

D How many multiplication sentences can you create for the product 36? Write all of the possible multiplication sentences below.

Hint

You could use blocks or beads to model arrays of 36.

Fast Facts

A You have to be fast to be a racer! Solve these multiplication facts as fast as Lightning McQueen races.

$2 \times 2 =$ _____ $3 \times 4 =$ _____ $5 \times 6 =$ _____

$8 \times 2 =$ _____ $7 \times 6 =$ _____ $4 \times 4 =$ _____

$5 \times 3 =$ _____ $3 \times 7 =$ _____ $2 \times 9 =$ _____

$2 \times 3 =$ _____ $0 \times 6 =$ _____ $8 \times 10 =$ _____

$8 \times 4 =$ _____ $4 \times 6 =$ _____ $3 \times 8 =$ _____

$5 \times 9 =$ _____ $10 \times 2 =$ _____ $5 \times 2 =$ _____

$3 \times 6 =$ _____ $4 \times 7 =$ _____ $5 \times 4 =$ _____

$9 \times 10 =$ _____ $3 \times 3 =$ _____ $8 \times 7 =$ _____

$0 \times 10 =$ _____ $9 \times 2 =$ _____ $5 \times 7 =$ _____

$4 \times 2 =$ _____ $5 \times 5 =$ _____ $8 \times 9 =$ _____

Going Backward

Miguel wants to go back to the Land of the Living. Going backward along a number line can help you divide.

A Use the number line to model division. Write a division sentence.

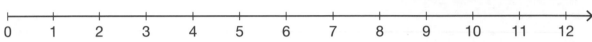

```
0   1   2   3   4   5   6   7   8   9   10  11  12
```

1. Start at 8 and jump backward by 2s to 0.

_____

2. Start at 10 and jump backward by 2s to 0.

_____

3. Start at 9 and jump backward by 3s to 0.

_____

4. Start at 8 and jump backward by 4s to 0.

_____

5. Start at 6 and jump backward by 3s to 0.

_____

Did You Know?

When you use a number line for division, the starting number is the dividend. The size of your backward jumps is your divisor. The number of jumps along the number line is your quotient.

B Choose one of the questions above. Label the dividend, divisor, and quotient.

C Use the number line to solve the division sentences.

```
|--+--+--+--+--+--+--+--+--+--+--+--+--+--+--+--+--+--+--+--+--+--+--+--+--+--+--+--+--+--→
0                    10                   20                   30
```

1. $21 \div 7 =$ _____

2. $15 \div 5 =$ _____

3. $16 \div 4 =$ _____

4. $18 \div 9 =$ _____

5. $25 \div 5 =$ _____

6. $14 \div 2 =$ _____

7. $24 \div 6 =$ _____

8. $20 \div 4 =$ _____

9. $30 \div 3 =$ _____

10. $21 \div 3 =$ _____

D Ernesto de la Cruz shows Miguel the guitars his fans sent him. There are 24 guitars placed in 3 rows.

1. How many guitars are in each row? _____

2. If the 24 guitars are rearranged in 4 rows, how many guitars would be in each row? _____

3. Write the division sentence for this new arrangement.

_____

4. Ernesto receives 4 more guitars. How many sets of 4 can now be made? Explain your answer.

_____

_____

Buy and Sell!

Andy's mom is having a yard sale and thinks about selling some of Andy's toys.

A Calculate how much a customer might pay for each combination.

$2.05

$3.75

1. Hamm and Rex _____

2. the Green Army Men and the Aliens _____

$4.99

3. Hamm and the Green Army Men _____

$1.50

4. Rex and the Aliens _____

Did You Know?

Any numbers to the right of the decimal are less than a whole dollar. Numbers to the left of the decimal are whole dollars.

B Compare the costs of different toys. Show your work. Explain your answer.

1. How much more does Rex cost than Hamm?

2. How much more do the Green Army Men cost than the Aliens?

_____

3. How much more does Rex cost than the Aliens?

_____

4. How much more do the Green Army Men cost than Hamm?

_____

C A neighbor wants to buy some toys. He has $7.00. Would he have enough money to buy Hamm, the Aliens, and Rex? Show your work. Explain your answer.

_____

_____

Luckily, Andy's mom does not sell any of Andy's beloved toys!

Again and Again

Patterns are everywhere in the Land of the Living.
They are everywhere in the Land of the Dead, too!

A Identify the **attributes** of each pattern using these
words: **size**, **color**, **orientation**, **shape**, **number**.

1.

_____

2.

_____

3.

_____

4.

_____

B Identify the attributes of each pattern.
Then, extend each pattern.

1.

_____

2.

_____

C Create your own pattern using three attributes.
Describe the attributes of your pattern.

_____

_____

Friends Rule!

Lightning McQueen enjoys hanging out with the Radiator Springs gang.

A Use this picture to complete each table. Then, write its pattern rule in the space provided.

1.

Number of Cars	Number of Wheels
1	4
2	
3	
4	

> **Did You Know?**
>
> You can use a **pattern rule** to relate the **term numbers** (first column) to values in the second column of the table. A pattern rule always includes the number you begin with and how much the pattern increases or decreases.

Pattern rule: _____

2.

Number of Cars	Number of Eyes
4	8
3	
2	
1	

> **Hint**
>
> Patterns can grow (addition) or shrink (subtraction).

Pattern rule: _____

B Follow the pattern rule to complete each table.

1. Start at 3 and increase by 4.

Term Number	Number in Pattern
1	3
2	
3	
4	

Hint

Use skip counting to complete the patterns.

2. Start at 25 and decrease by 5.

Term Number	Number in Pattern
1	
2	
3	
4	

C Create your own pattern and pattern rule.

Pattern rule: _____

_____

Term Number	Number in Pattern
1	
2	
3	
4	

Studying Graphs

Mike and Sulley love being students at Monsters University!

A Mike and Sulley study 3 hours each day.

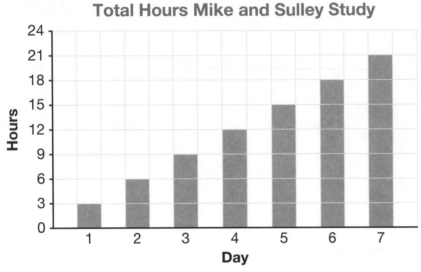

Total Hours Mike and Sulley Study

Hint

The total number of hours Mike and Sulley study is the number of hours studied for that day and all previous days combined.

1. Complete the table to show the total number of hours Mike and Sulley study.

Day	1	2	3	4	5	6	7
Total Hours Mike and Sulley Study	3	6					

2. Write the pattern rule.

_____

B Mike and Sulley study for 5 more days.
Extend the number pattern by 5 more days.

Day	8	9	10	11	12
Total Hours Mike and Sulley Study					

C Complete a bar graph to represent the total number of hours Mike and Sulley study from day 8 to day 12.

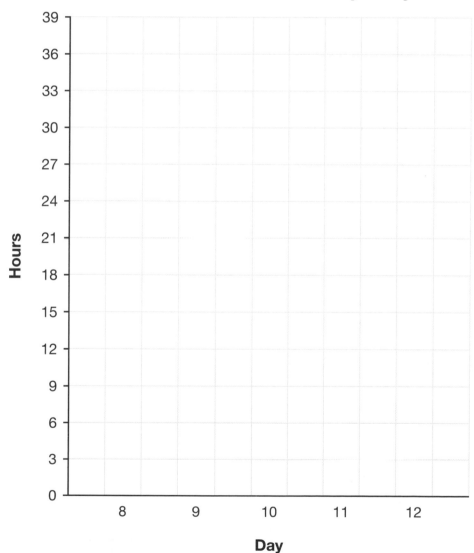

Total Hours Mike and Sulley Study

What's Missing?

Woody and Forky are missing! Buzz is looking for them. In addition and subtraction, numbers sometimes go missing, too!

A Find the missing number for each subtraction sentence.

1	2	3	4	5	6	7	8	9	10
11	12	13	14	15	16	17	18	19	20
21	22	23	24	25	26	27	28	29	30
31	32	33	34	35	36	37	38	39	40
41	42	43	44	45	46	47	48	49	50
51	52	53	54	55	56	57	58	59	60
61	62	63	64	65	66	67	68	69	70
71	72	73	74	75	76	77	78	79	80
81	82	83	84	85	86	87	88	89	90
91	92	93	94	95	96	97	98	99	100

1. $23 - \underline{\hspace{2cm}} = 21$

2. $29 - \underline{\hspace{2cm}} = 14$

3. $84 - \underline{\hspace{2cm}} = 62$

4. $73 - \underline{\hspace{2cm}} = 59$

5. $57 - \underline{\hspace{2cm}} = 38$

6. $63 - \underline{\hspace{2cm}} = 41$

7. $\underline{\hspace{2cm}} - 20 = 47$

8. $\underline{\hspace{2cm}} - 9 = 35$

Hint

When the second number is missing, add up from the answer to the first number. If the first number is missing, add the second number and the answer. A 100-chart can help you with this.

B Find the missing number for each addition sentence.

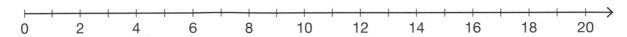

1. $6 +$ _____ $= 9$ 2. $9 +$ _____ $= 14$

3. _____ $+ 5 = 16$ 4. _____ $+ 3 = 10$

Hint

Use the number line to help you.

5. $7 +$ _____ $= 18$ 6. _____ $+ 12 = 20$

7. $6 +$ _____ $= 11$ 8. _____ $+ 17 = 19$

9. _____ $+ 7 = 17$ 10. _____ $+ 8 = 12$

C Bonnie buys a roll of star stickers. The roll has 57 stickers. When she gets home, she counts only 33 stickers. How many stickers went missing? Write the number sentence and explain your answer.

_____

_____

_____

_____

_____

_____

One or None

Many monsters at Monsters University do not have tails. Ms. Squibbles doesn't have one either!

A Write a multiplication fact for the number of tails in each example. The first one is done for you.

1. $3 \times 0 = 0$

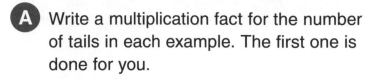

2. _____

3. _____

4. _____

5. What do you notice when you multiply a number by 0?

   _____

B Mike thinks monsters with one eye are the best-looking monsters. Write a multiplication fact for the number of eyes in each example.

1. _____

2. _____

3. _____

4.

_____

5. What pattern do you notice when you multiply a number by 1?

_____

C Calculate each multiplication sentence.

1. $1 \times 20 =$ _____

2. $41 \times 1 =$ _____

3. $0 \times 420 =$ _____

4. $1 \times 934 =$ _____

Who's the Tallest?

A Use your finger or hand to estimate the height of each toy. Then, measure its height with a ruler.

1.

Estimate: _____ in.

Measurement: _____ in.

2.

Estimate: _____ in.

Measurement: _____ in.

3.

Estimate: _____ cm

Measurement: _____ cm

4.

Estimate: _____ cm

Measurement: _____ cm

5. Which toy is the tallest?

_____

B Estimate and measure other items in inches.

1. width of this book   Estimate: _____   Measurement: _____

2. length of this book   Estimate: _____   Measurement: _____

3. height of the Hint box   Estimate: _____   Measurement: _____

C Find objects at home that you estimate have lengths of 20 cm, 40 cm, and 60 cm. Then, use a ruler to measure them.

1. 20 cm   Object: _____   Exact measurement: _____

2. 40 cm   Object: _____   Exact measurement: _____

3. 60 cm   Object: _____   Exact measurement: _____

4. Explain how you estimated the length of each object.

_____

_____

5. Which of your estimates came closest to the actual measurement?

_____

_____

_____

_____

Made to Measure

Mike packs everything he needs for school, including a ruler!

 Draw the objects listed below. Use Mike's ruler to help you.

```
INCHES    1       2       3       4       5       6
```

1. A pencil that is $3\frac{1}{4}$ in. long.

2. A monster that is $5\frac{1}{2}$ in. long.

3. An eraser that is 2 in. long.

4. A straw that is $4\frac{3}{4}$ in. long.

B Use a ruler to measure the height of each monster's class photo. Number these photos in order from **shortest** to **tallest**. The first one is done for you.

_1_ in. (1)

Mike

____ in. ( )

Art

____ in. ( )

Nan

____ in. ( )

Dean Hardscrabble

____ in. ( )

Don

____ in. ( )

Sulley

How Heavy Is a Scare Pig?

Archie the Scare Pig steals Mike's Monsters University hat! Mike tries to stop him from getting away, but Archie is stronger and heavier than Mike thought.

Archie's **mass** can be measured in pounds or kilograms. Mike's hat can be measured in ounces or grams.

A Choose a unit of measurement for each item. (Circle) your choice.

Did You Know?

There are 1,000 grams in 1 kilogram (kg). A gram is about the weight of a paper clip. A dictionary has a mass of about 1 kilogram.

1. suitcase   grams   kilograms

2. Scare Games flyer   ounces   pounds

3. backpack   grams   kilograms

4. movie ticket   ounces   pounds

5. map   grams   kilograms

6. textbook   ounces   pounds

B Think about the mass for each animal.

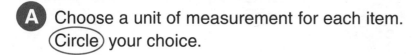

elephant   blue whale   robin   lion

human adult male   bee   wolf

B These are some objects you might find in your own home. (Circle) the object that has a capacity closest to 1 liter.

1.

2.

3.

4.

5.

C List two objects for each question.

1. Which objects in your home have a mass of about 2 pounds?

_____

2. Which objects in your home have a capacity of about 1 liter?

_____

Measure Up!

Héctor, Dante, and Miguel are performing on stage. The crowd can see that the friends are all different heights. Miguel is shorter than Héctor, but taller than Dante.

A Choose the most likely unit of measurement for each item. (Circle) your choice.

1. Miguel's height

   4 cm   4 ft.   4 m

2. length of Miguel's guitar

   1 cm   1 in.   1 m

3. length of Miguel's thumb

   4 cm   4 in.   4 m

4. length of Miguel's hand

   10 cm   10 in.   10 m

5. length of Héctor's arm

   31 ft.   31 cm   31 in.

6. length of Héctor's nose

   4 m   4 cm   4 ft.

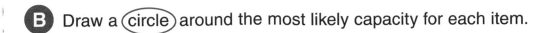

B Draw a (circle) around the most likely capacity for each item.

1. juice box	20 mL	200 mL	2 L
2. pop can	35 mL	350 mL	3 L
3. carton of milk	1 L	3 L	10 L
4. bottle of soda	10 mL	2 L	10 L
5. drinking cup	10 mL	200 mL	1 L
6. spoon	5 mL	50 mL	500 mL
7. swimming pool	5 L	50 L	5000 L
8. large cooking pot	2 mL	200 mL	4 L
9. tube of toothpaste	10 mL	100 mL	1 L
10. bottle of dish soap	1 mL	1 L	10 L

Hint

Use items you know to help you visualize capacity. For example, a bottle of water is 500 mL.

C Answer the following questions.

1. What happens when you pour 1 gallon of milk into a 2 quart measuring cup?

_____

_____

2. If your garden needs 1 L of water each day and your watering can holds 250 mL, how many times do you have to fill up your watering can?

_____

Catch Me If You Can!

Lightning enjoys driving around the **perimeter** of a track. Sometimes, he moves so fast that it looks like he is covering the whole **area** of the track at once.

A Calculate the perimeter of each shape. Then calculate the area. Each square on the grid represents 1 in².

Did You Know?

The formula for **perimeter** is 2 lengths + 2 widths or P = *l* + *l* + *w* + *w*. The formula for **area** is length × width or A = *l* × *w*. Its measurement is squared (²), for example, 10 in².

1.

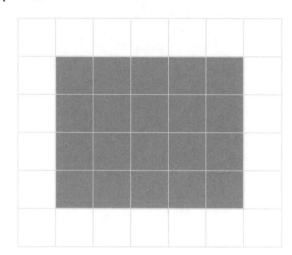

P = _____   A = _____

2.

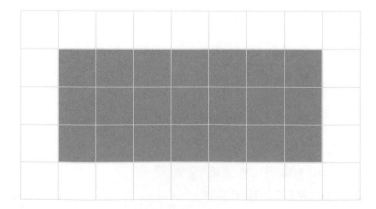

P = _____   A = _____

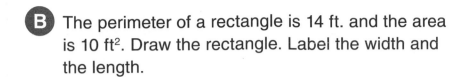

B The perimeter of a rectangle is 14 ft. and the area is 10 ft^2. Draw the rectangle. Label the width and the length.

C Lightning races around a track with an area of 24 m^2. Write all combinations of length and width that will equal an area of 24 m^2.

It's All about the Volume

Sulley has one textbook that is so big it might not fit in his backpack!

A Calculate the **volume** of each book.

1.
   4 cm
   3 cm
   5 cm

   _____

Did You Know?

Volume is the space taken up by a 3-D object. The formula for volume is length × width × height or $V = l \times w \times h$. Its measurement is cubed (^{3}). For example, $V = 2 \times 3 \times 4 = 24$ cm^3.

2. 2 cm
   5 cm   10 cm

   _____

3. 5 cm
   6 cm   3 cm

   _____

4. 2 cm
   7 cm   9 cm

   _____

5. 4 cm
   8 cm   3 cm

   _____

B Complete the measurements table. Calculate Volume #1 using the first set of dimensions. Calculate Volume #2 using the change in dimension.

Changing Measurements

	Original Dimensions			Volume #1	Change	Volume #2
	Length	Width	Height			
1.	3 in.	4 in.	6 in.		height to 3 in.	
2.	5 cm	2 cm	8 cm		length to 10 cm	
3.	2 in.	4 in.	3 in.		width to 2 in.	
4.	3 ft.	8 ft.	2 ft.		length to 6 ft.	
5.	4 m	3 m	5 m		height to 10 m	

C Write a sentence to answer each question.

1. What happens to the volume when a dimension is doubled?

_____

_____

2. What happens to the volume when a dimension is halved?

_____

_____

Good Timing

The toys are planning a schedule of activities while Bonnie is at school.

A Match the timed activity with the clock showing the correct time.

1. March around the room.
   9:05

2. Play hide-and-seek in Bonnie's drawer.
   10:30

3. Jump off the bed.
   11:10

4. Practice lasso skills.
   11:35

5. Stack blocks.
   12:15

6. Clean up.
   12:50

B Show the correct time on each blank clock.

1.

2.

3.

4.

5.

6.

7.

8.

9.

10.

C What is the difference between 6 a.m. and 6 p.m.?

_____

_____

_____

_____

Hint

Reading minutes on a clock is like skip counting by 5s.

Simply Symmetrical

Lightning McQueen enters the Crazy Eight demolition derby.

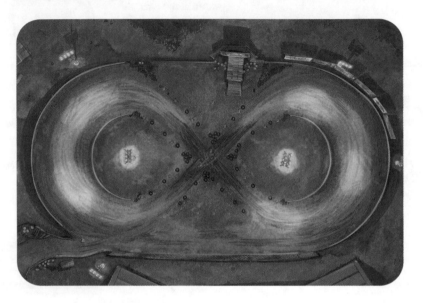

A Examine the Crazy Eight Track. Draw any **lines of symmetry**.

B Examine each image. Draw any lines of symmetry. Circle the image that has no lines of symmetry.

1.

2.

3.

4.

C Draw lines of symmetry on the shapes below.
Describe the lines of symmetry. The first one is
done for you.

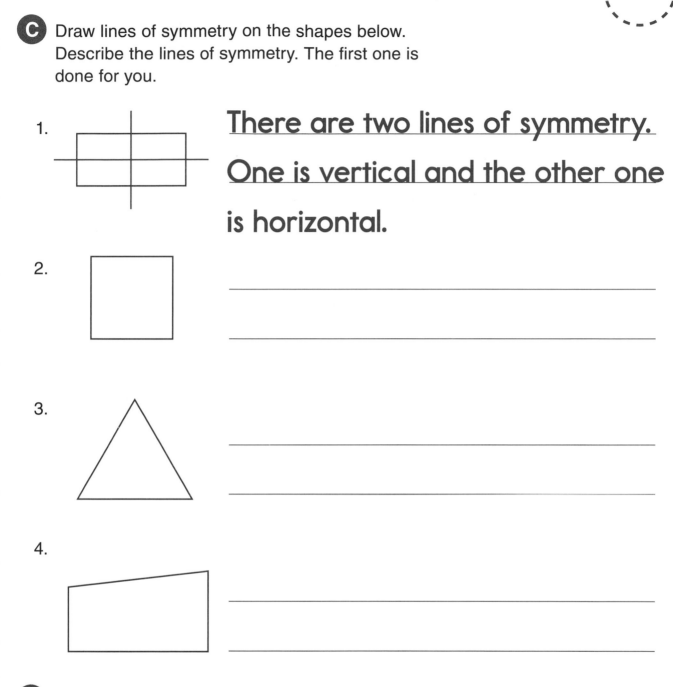

1. There are two lines of symmetry. One is vertical and the other one is horizontal.

2. _____

_____

3. _____

_____

4. _____

_____

D Draw a symmetrical object. Show the lines of
symmetry. Describe the lines of symmetry.

_____

Shape Up!

The Green Army Men defend the block castle from a fire-breathing dragon, played by Rex. What shapes can you identify in the castle?

A Match each name to the correct shape.

1. pentagon

2. square

3. triangle

4. octagon

5. heptagon

6. rectangle

7. hexagon

B Use the shapes to complete the Venn diagrams. Write the letters representing the shapes in the Venn diagrams.

1. **Four Sides or More   Two Lines of Symmetry**

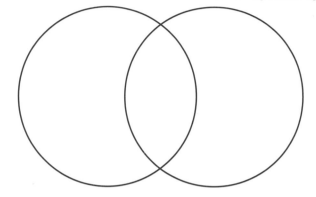

2. **Four Right Angles   Equal Side Lengths**

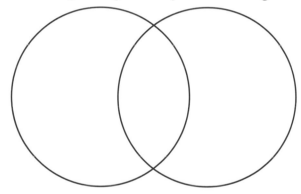

3. **Four Sides   Equal Side Lengths**

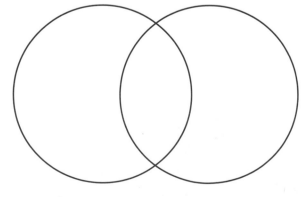

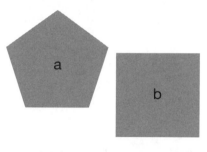

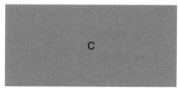

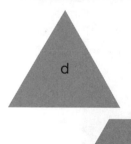

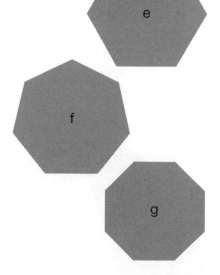

Mirror Images

This guitar is shown in a **vertical reflection**.

Here, the guitar is shown in a **horizontal reflection**.

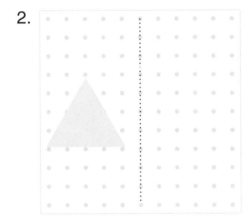

A Trace the dotted line to show the vertical line of reflection. Draw a vertical reflection of each picture.

1.

2.

3.

4.

B Trace the dotted horizontal line of reflection. Draw a horizontal reflection of each picture.

1.
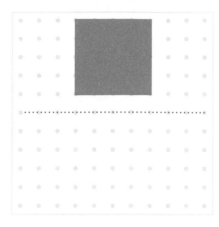

2.
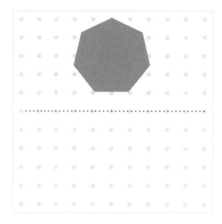

3.
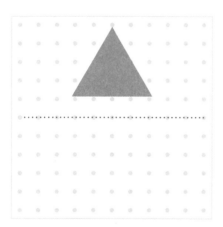

4.
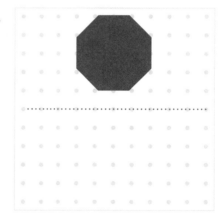

C Trace the vertical line of reflection. Reflect this image vertically. Now, trace the horizontal line of reflection. Reflect this image horizontally.

1.
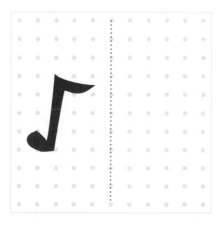

2.

That's the Point!

Mike arrives at the Oozma Kappa fraternity house with his suitcases. His suitcases are rectangular **prisms**, with **edges** and **vertices**.

A Complete the table.

3-D Object	Number of Edges	Number of Vertices
rectangular prism		
cube		
triangular prism		
rectangular pyramid		

Did You Know?

Prisms are 3-D objects that have rectangular **faces**, or sides. They have 2 ends that are the same. **Pyramids** are 3-D objects that have 1 rectangular or triangular face at the base, and all other faces are triangular. An **edge** is the line where 2 faces meet on a 3-D object. A **vertex** is a point where two or more lines meet.

Hint

The plural of vertex is **vertices**.

B Use Venn diagrams to compare the features of different 3-D objects.

1. **Rectangular Pyramid**　　**Rectangular Prism**

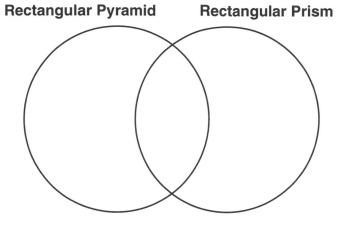

2. **Rectangular Prism**　　**Cube**

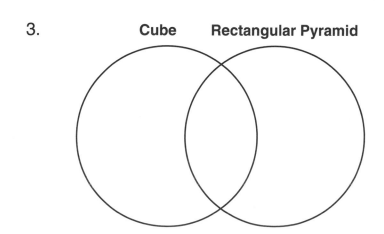

3. **Cube**　　**Rectangular Pyramid**

Building Boxes

Lightning McQueen's products are boxed and ready for sale. The boxes are rectangular prisms. They are built using **nets**.

A Match each prism to its net.

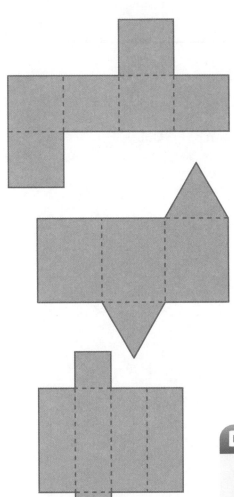

1.

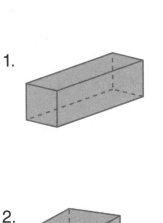

2.

3.

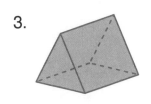

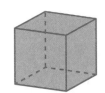

Did You Know?

A **net** is a flat shape that folds to create a 3-D object.

B Which objects in your home were built using nets? List two objects.

C Follow these instructions to build a box for Lightning's newest product.

1. Trace the net onto a blank piece of paper.

2. Cut out the net along the solid lines.

3. Fold along the dashed lines.

4. Tape the edges.

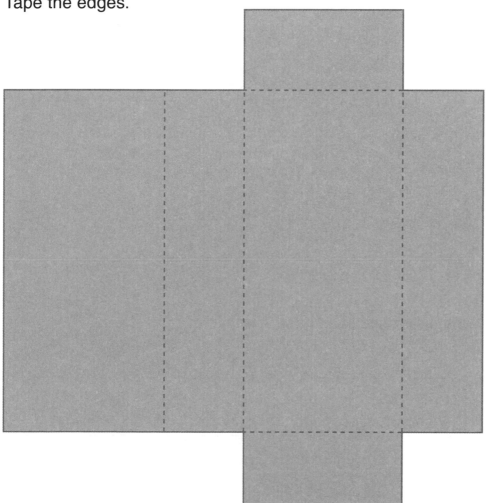

On the Move

The toys are playing hide-and-seek in Bonnie's room.
Help Woody find them using this grid map.

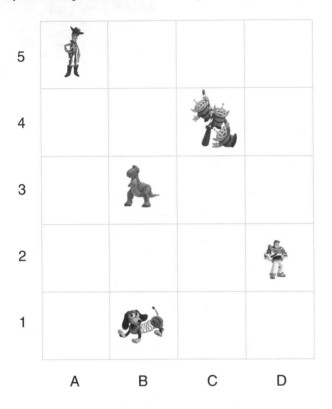

Hint

Use words like **left**,
right, **up**, and **down** to
describe movement on
a grid.

A Describe one route for each instruction. The first
one is done for you.

1. Woody to Slinky Dog

Woody moves right one space and down four spaces.

2. Rex to Buzz

_____

3. Aliens to Rex

_____

4. Woody to Buzz

_____

5. Woody to Rex to Aliens

_____

6. Rex to Slinky Dog

_____

7. Aliens to Buzz

_____

8. Rex to Buzz to Slinky Dog

_____

9. Slinky Dog to Aliens

_____

B Woody wants to find each toy. Describe one
continuous route that will take him to each toy.

_____

_____

_____

_____

What Are the Chances?

The foreman at Monsters, Inc. does not know whom to choose for the next scare job. He could use a spinner.

A Examine the spinner on the right. Use these probability words to predict which monster will be chosen: **certain**, **likely**, **unlikely**, **equally likely**, **impossible**.

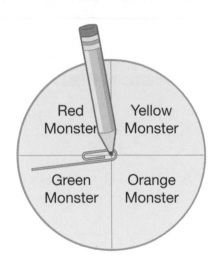

1. probability of choosing Orange Monster

_____

2. probability of choosing Yellow Monster or Orange Monster

_____

3. probability of choosing Red Monster or Green Monster

_____

4. probability of spinning Purple Monster

_____

5. probability of spinning Orange, Yellow, Red, or Green Monster

_____

B If you spin the spinner below 10 times, how many times do you predict you will spin a number less than 4?

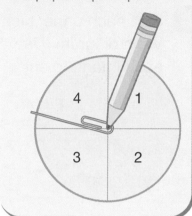

_____

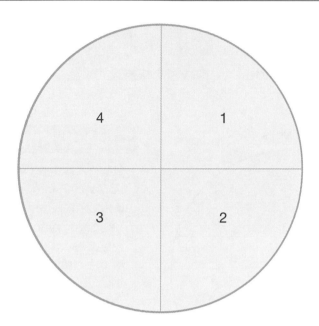

1. Use a probability word to describe the probability of spinning a number less than 4 in 10 spins.

_____

2. Spin the spinner 10 times. Record your results using a tally chart.

3. Did your prediction match the results of your experiment? Why, or why not?

_____

_____

Sort It Out

The *papel picado* banners that hang in Miguel's village for *Día de los Muertos* come in many designs and colors.

A Sort each papel picado banner into the Venn diagram. Use the numbers beside each image to sort.

Purple   Flowers

1.

2.

3.

4.

5.

B Sort each character into the Venn diagram. Use the numbers beside each character's name to sort.

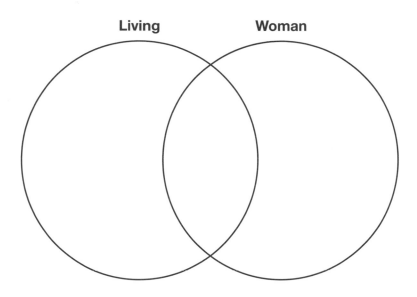

Living   Woman

1. PapáJulio

2. Mamá Imelda

3. Abuelita

4. Dante

5. Miguel

6. Tía Gloria

Label It!

The Legends practiced often for a race.

A This **bar graph** compares the number of practice wins for each car.

1. Add labels to this graph.

Practice Wins for the Legends

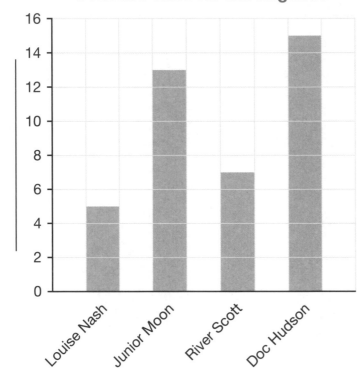

_____

2. Who had the most wins? Who had the least?

_____

3. What is the scale of this graph? _____

B The Next Generation racers have their practice races on simulators. This bar graph compares the number of practice race wins for the Next Generation racers.

1. Add a title and labels to this graph.

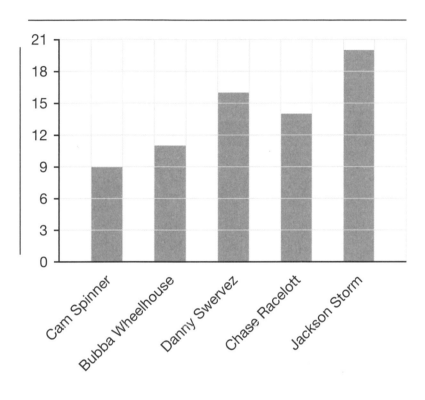

2. What title did you choose? Why?

_____

3. Who has the most wins? Who has the least?

_____

4. What is the scale of this graph? _____

Picture It!

On Monday, Dante collects 20 bones. On Tuesday, he collects 30 bones. On Wednesday, he collects 25 bones. On Thursday and Friday, he collects 15 bones each day.

A Use the above information to complete the **pictograph**.

Title: _____

Monday

Tuesday

_____

_____

_____

Each  means 5 bones.

B Draw a pictograph for the data below.

Shoes Made in the Rivera Workshop

Monday	8 shoes
Tuesday	12 shoes
Wednesday	10 shoes
Thursday	6 shoes
Friday	9 shoes

Title: _____

Hint
Draw half a shoe to represent 1 shoe.

Monday

Tuesday

Wednesday

Thursday

Friday

Each 👞 means 2 shoes.

Interpret It!

Fans have packed the stadium to watch their favorite teams compete in the Scare Games.

A Read this bar graph about the number of fans at Scare Games events.

1. What is the scale of the graph?

_____

2. List the events from most fans to least fans.

_____

_____

_____

_____

_____

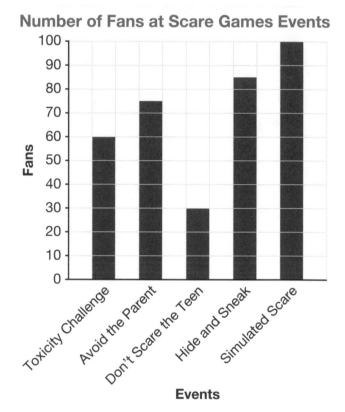

Number of Fans at Scare Games Events

3. How do you know which event has the most fans?

_____

_____

B Read this pictograph.

Number of Teams' Fans at the Toxicity Challenge

Oozma Kappa

Roar Omega Roar

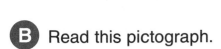

Jaws Theta Chi

Eta Hiss Hiss

Python Nu Kappa

Each  means 2 fans.

1. How many fans does each team have?

   Oozma Kappa _____   Roar Omega Roar _____

   Jaws Theta Chi _____   Eta Hiss Hiss _____

   Python Nu Kappa _____

2. What other scale could be used?

   _____

Graph It!

Bonnie has many different kinds of toys that she plays with all the time.

A Bonnie has 3 metal toys, 9 animal toys, 6 space toys, and 15 plastic toys.

1. Complete the bar graph to show this data.

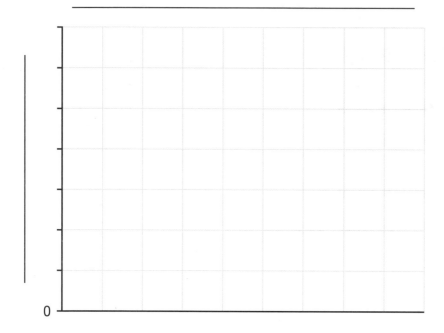

0

Hint

Remember that a bar graph needs a title, scale, axes labels, and bar labels.

2. Why did you choose this title?

3. Why did you choose this scale?

B Bonnie plays with Dolly and Jessie for 6 hours each. She plays with Woody and Buzz for 2 hours each. She plays with Trixie for 3 hours.

Hint
Use a ruler to create the bars on your graph.

1. Draw a bar graph to show this data.

2. Why did you choose this title?

_____

3. Why did you choose these labels for your axes?

_____

4. Why did you choose this scale?

_____

Language Arts

Word Knowledge

- Make your own idiom! Explain what it means. Use it in a sentence.

- Make a list of the abbreviations you know. Maybe it's for your address or a saying you know.

Writing

- The next time you want to ask a parent or guardian to do something, write a persuasive argument. List reasons and use logical thinking.

- Think about different ways to say things. Ask yourself, "How can we rephrase that?" during everyday activities. Make a game out of it! How would a pirate say that? How would Mike and Sulley say that?

- Rewrite favorite stories with different endings! Practice creative thinking and problem solving by asking new questions in the context of the story.

Comprehension

- Start to diversify your reading with fictional stories, dramas, and poetry, as well as nonfiction stories about history or science.

- Read a book and watch a movie! Make connections between the two and practice more complex thinking.

- Combine knowledge of letter sounds, syllables, base words, and affixes to tackle unfamiliar words. Use flash cards to make a game out of it by creating words from pieces.

- Get comfortable talking about your ideas with a parent or guardian. Sit down after reading or watching something and discuss. Talk about your thoughts.

- Tell a story about your day to a parent or guardian to practice organization and fluency.

- Make a scavenger hunt using different reference materials. Choose a word to look up in the dictionary. Then, search for it elsewhere: in other text, online, on purchased products, etc. to find more information.

Math

Number and Operations

- Work more on fractions. Draw and decorate *Día de los Muertos* skulls. Play around with fractions. Quiz yourself by asking what fraction of the skulls have black eyes, have blue in them, etc.

- Practice rounding to the nearest ten or hundred. Quiz yourself with numbers like 355. What nearest hundred should the number be rounded to?

- Practice multiplication. Find the number of legs to cats, wheels to bikes, feet to person. Quiz yourself with questions like, "If there are 3 cats, how many legs are there?"

Patterns and Algebra

- Create number patterns based on addition, subtraction, multiplication, and division. Take turns with a parent or guardian coming up with a pattern while the other person solves it.

- Look for patterns in nature and around your home.

Data and Probability

- Track your family's breakfasts: record the breakfasts of every person for 5 days. After the 5 days of data collection, create a bar graph. Write all the foods eaten at the bottom of a bar graph. Make dashes on the vertical axis showing the number of times each breakfast was eaten. Draw bars to show which breakfast was most popular. Share your results!

Geometry

- Find a cardboard box that you can take apart. Use it as a model for a 3-D net. Make your own net for a 3-D object.

- Go on a walk around your neighborhood or town with your parent or guardian. Point out different structures, trees, and objects that have definable shapes. Ask your parent or guardian if they see any more shapes.

Measurement

- Using a ruler, find objects that are about a foot long and measure them. Try measuring to the nearest fourth of an inch. Record your findings and compare lengths.

- Ask a parent or guardian for help measuring yourself. Then, help your parent or guardian measure themselves. Find the difference between heights.

- Time how long it takes you to do routine tasks like brushing teeth, taking a shower, eating breakfast, and getting dressed. When each task time has been recorded, figure out what time you need to wake up and do each task if you have to leave at 8:00.

Glossary

abbreviation: shortened form of a word; words that are often abbreviated are days, months, parts of addresses, and measurements (cm = centimeter).

abstract noun: noun that names a feeling, concept, or idea.

action verbs: words that describe something that can be done or something that can be done in the mind, such as *enjoy*, *assume*, *think*.

adverb: word that describes a verb; it tells how, where, or when an action is done.

antonym: word meaning the opposite of another word.

area: the measurement of the space inside an object's perimeter. The formula for rectangular area is length $\times$ width, or $A = l \times w$.

array: rectangular arrangement of items in rows and columns to make it easier to multiply or divide.

attribute: feature that you can describe, such as shape, size, number, color, and orientation.

base word: gives a word its basic meaning.

capacity: amount a container will hold.

comparing adjective: adjective used to compare two or more nouns (*faster*, *fastest*).

conjunction: word that connects sentences or phrases; common conjunctions include: *for*, *and*, *nor*, *but*, *or*, *yet*, *so*.

denominator: bottom number in a fraction; it shows how many equal parts a whole is divided into.

dividend: number that is to be divided by another number.

divisor: number that is used to divide another number.

edge: line where two faces meet on a 3-D object.

equivalent: having the same amount or value.

evaluating texts: reading strategy that readers use to think about what they liked in the text, what they didn't like, whether the author's ideas make sense, and if they have any questions after reading the text.

fable: short piece of fiction that teaches a lesson, or moral. A fable usually has one to three characters; the characters are usually animals or plants that can talk.

face: 2-D shape that is a flat side of a 3-D object.

factor: number used to multiply.

friendly number strategy: a strategy for addition or subtraction where equations are mentally shifted around to make them easier to work with. For example, 9 + 7 can be shifted mentally to create a tens problem, 10 + 6, which is easier to solve. The same strategy can be used for recognizable doubles equations. For 7 + 8, we know 8 + 8 is 16 and 7 is one less, so the answer is 15.

idiom: expression that doesn't really mean what the words say; idioms are a type of figurative language.

line of symmetry: line that divides an object so that what is on one side of the line is the same as what is on the other side.

mass: amount of matter in an object.

numerator: top number in a fraction; it shows the number of parts we have.

perimeter: the boundary line around a closed geometric figure. The formula for rectangular perimeter is 2 lengths + 2 widths, or $P = l + l + w + w$.

pictograph: a way of showing data using images.

possessive adjective: word that describes the noun that follows it, describing specifically who or what the noun belongs to (*my*, *your*, *her*, *his*, *its*, *our*, *their*).

possessive pronoun: word that describes ownership and is used instead of a noun (*mine*, *yours*, *his*, *hers*, *ours*, *yours*, *theirs*).

prism: 3-D object with identical bases.

product: answer to a multiplication sentence.

proper noun: word that names a specific person, place, or thing; it is capitalized, even if it is not at the start of a sentence.

pyramid: 3-D object with one rectangular or triangular face at the base, and all other faces are triangles that meet at a point.

quotient: answer to a division sentence.

reflection: moving a shape so that it looks like it is being reflected in a mirror.

scale: value that represents the number of items for each symbol in a graph. For example, in a bar graph, the scale tells you by how much each interval on the *y*-axis increases. In a pictograph, the scale is the number of items that each symbol represents.

sequence word: word that helps put events in the order in which they happen. Some sequence words include: *second*, *before*, *after*, *while*, *during*.

summarize: briefly describe the most important parts of a text in your own words.

syllable: word part that has one vowel sound, with or without consonants surrounding the vowel.

synonym: word that has the same or nearly the same meaning as another.

term number: number of times a pattern repeats.

verb tense: form of verbs that express a time frame—past, present, or future. Verbs in the present tense describe an action that is happening right now. (I *play* soccer.) The past tense of a verb describes an action that has already happened. (I *played* soccer.) The future tense of a verb uses a helping verb like *will* with the base form of a verb. (I *will play* soccer.)

vertices: more than one vertex.

vertex: corner or point where lines meet.

volume: the space taken up by a 3-D object. The formula for volume of rectangular prisms is length $\times$ width $\times$ height, or $V = l \times w \times h$.

Count 'em!

The name Mike has one **syllable**. The name Sul / ley has two syllables. The word Mon / stro / po / lis has four syllables!

A Say each word. Draw slashes to separate each word into syllables. Write the number of syllables in each word. The first one is done for you.

1. mon/ster __2__
2. chil/dren __2__
3. scare __1__
4. fac/tor/y __3__
5. me/chan/i/cal __4__
6. col/lec/tor __3__
7. clos/et __2__
8. scream __1__
9. friend/ship __2__
10. build/ings __2__
11. team/mates __2__
12. night/time __2__
13. worked __1__
14. scar/ing __2__
15. se/cre/tive __3__
16. en/e/my __3__

Did You Know?
Words have parts called **syllables**. Every syllable has a vowel sound. The number of vowel sounds you hear in a word is the number of syllables.

Hint
Clap each syllable as you say a word. The claps will help you hear and count the syllables.

B Write a sentence using at least three two-syllable words.

Answers will vary.
For example, Mike and Sulley's friendship is
very strong.

6

C Fill in the table.

1. Sort these words into the table.

machine   conveyor   company
light   Boo   energy
worker   friends   safe
Randall   helper   passageway

One Syllable	Two Syllables	Three Syllables
light	ma/chine	con/vey/or
Boo	work/er	com/pa/ny
friends	Ran/dall	en/er/gy
safe	help/er	pas/sage/way
	Answers will vary.	

2. Draw slashes to separate each two-syllable and three-syllable word into syllables.

3. Add your own word to each column in the table.

7

Consonant Crew

Like Lightning McQueen's pit crew, some consonants work as a team.

A Complete each of the following words, which all have a consonant blend. Say the word. Listen for the blend.

1. scr   squ   **str** __str__ing
2. sm   fl   cr   __sm__ile
3. fr   sk   spl   __spl__ash
4. ng   nt   rk   pare__nt__
5. st   nd   bl   du__st__
6. tr   scr   fr   __fr__uit
7. gl   gr   cr   __gl__ue
8. lp   ng   rst   fi__rst__

Did You Know?
Consonant **blends** are two or three consonants that work together to make a blended sound. In a blend, you can hear each consonant sound, like **fl** in fly and **str** in street.

B Underline the consonant blends in these sentences.

1. Guido is a <u>bl</u>ue fo<u>rk</u>li<u>ft</u>.

2. Luigi and Guido are be<u>st</u> <u>fr</u>iends.

3. Luigi's shop has many tools, like <u>scr</u>ew<u>dr</u>ivers and <u>r</u>a<u>tch</u>ets.

8

C Complete each sentence by selecting the most suitable consonant blend.

spr   dr   rk   sp   scr   tr

1. Lightning __dr__eams of winning races.

2. Racing takes practice and hard wo__rk__.

3. On dirt racetracks, the cars __spr__ay mud everywhere.

4. Smokey helps Lightning get ready to race on the __tr__ack.

5. The cars race at a very high __sp__eed.

6. Sometimes tires make a __scr__eeching sound.

Hint
Try each of the blends with each word to find a match.

D Write a word for each of the consonant blends.

str   fr   cl

1. _____
2. ___ Answers will vary. ___
3. _____

9

Consonant Combo

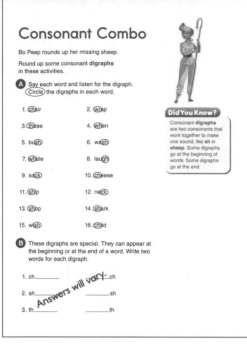

Bo Peep rounds up her missing sheep.

Round up some consonant **digraphs** in these activities.

A Say each word and listen for the digraph. Circle the digraphs in each word.

1. (ch)air
2. (wr)ap
3. (th)ese
4. (wh)en
5. bu(sh)
6. wa(sh)
7. (wh)ale
8. lau(gh)
9. so(ck)
10. (ch)eese
11. (sh)ip
12. ne(ck)
13. (sh)op
14. (sh)ark
15. wi(sh)
16. (ch)ild

Did You Know?

Consonant **digraphs** are two consonants that work together to make one sound, like **sh** in **sheep**. Some digraphs go at the beginning of words. Some digraphs go at the end.

B These digraphs are special. They can appear at the beginning or at the end of a word. Write two words for each digraph.

1. ch_____ _____ch
2. sh_____ _____sh   *Answers will vary.*
3. th_____ _____th

10

C Add a consonant digraph to each word to solve each riddle.

th   ck   wh   sh   ch   wr

1. The opposite of right: __wr__ong
2. Do this to a soccer ball: ki__ck__
3. Body part under your mouth: __ch__in
4. The color of Bo Peep's sheep: __wh__ite
5. Brush these to prevent cavities: tee__th__
6. These have fins and scales: fi__sh__

D Read the poem below. Underline the consonant digraphs.

Bo Peep's <u>sh</u>eep are lost. Will <u>th</u>ey start to cry?

All the toys want to help—<u>th</u>ey have to try!

But wait, <u>wh</u>at have <u>th</u>ey found?

<u>Th</u>e sheep are in a basket, safe and sound!

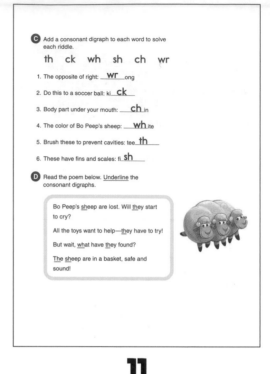

11

Did You Hear That?

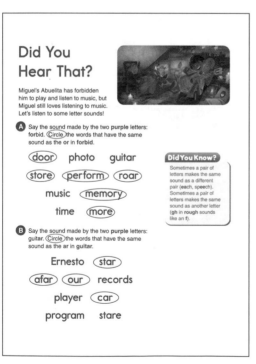

Miguel's Abuelita has forbidden him to play and listen to music, but Miguel still loves listening to music. Let's listen to some letter sounds!

A Say the sound made by the two purple letters: forbid. Circle the words that have the same sound as the or in forbid.

(door) photo guitar
(store) (perform) (roar)
music (memory)
time (more)

Did You Know?

Sometimes a pair of letters makes the same sound as a different pair (e**ach**, spee**ch**). Sometimes a pair of letters makes the same sound as another letter (gh in rough sounds like an f).

B Say the sound made by the two purple letters: guitar. Circle the words that have the same sound as the ar in guitar.

Ernesto (star)
(afar) (our) records
player (car)
program stare

12

C Say each word. Circle the word that does not make the same sound as the purple letter or letters. The first one is done for you.

1. offer   (highway)   phone   tough
2. this   then   feather   (otter)
3. late   raise   (stack)   eight
4. bring   young   (engine)   something
5. fine   kite   try   (kid)
6. book   (know)   candle   like
7. circle   seed   cell   (call)
8. dream   (wet)   week   eagle
9. plate   pack   apple   (phone)
10. grass   giggle   (giant)   grow

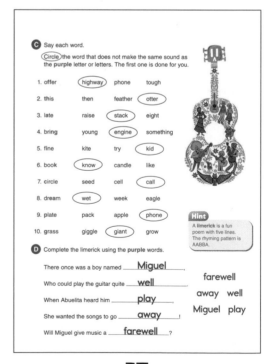

Hint

A **limerick** is a fun poem with five lines. The rhyming pattern is AABBA.

D Complete the limerick using the purple words.

There once was a boy named __Miguel__

Who could play the guitar quite __well__.

When Abuelita heard him __play__

She wanted the songs to go __away__!

Will Miguel give music a __farewell__?

farewell
away   well
Miguel   play

13

Winner or Whiner?

Vowels can have a short sound or a long sound.

The **u** in Junior is a long vowel. The **u** in Hudson is a short vowel.

Say their names to hear the difference.

A Say each word in the left-hand column. Identify whether the sound of the purple letter in each word is long or short. (Circle) your choice.

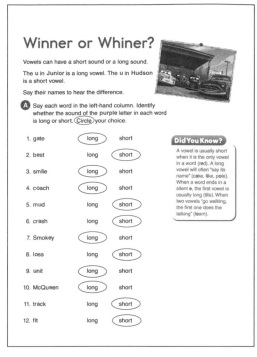

1. gate	(long)	short
2. best	long	(short)
3. smile	(long)	short
4. coach	(long)	short
5. mud	long	(short)
6. crash	long	(short)
7. Smokey	(long)	short
8. loss	long	(short)
9. unit	(long)	short
10. McQueen	(long)	short
11. track	long	(short)
12. fit	long	(short)

Did You Know?

A vowel is usually short when it is the only vowel in a word (red). A long vowel will often "say its name" (cake, like, pole). When a word ends in a silent e, the first vowel is usually long (tile). When two vowels "go walking," the first one does the talking" (team).

14

B Say each word that Natalie Certain and Chick Hicks use in their broadcast. Is the **purple** letter in each word a long vowel or a short vowel? Sort the words into the correct column of the chart.

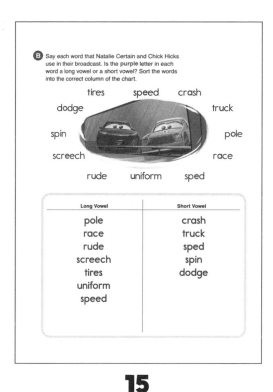

tires   speed   crash

dodge   truck

spin   pole

screech   race

rude   uniform   sped

Long Vowel	Short Vowel
pole	crash
race	truck
rude	sped
screech	spin
tires	dodge
uniform	
speed	

15

All in the Family

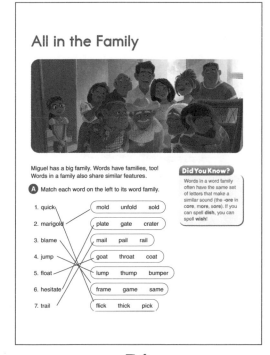

Miguel has a big family. Words have families, too! Words in a family also share similar features.

A Match each word on the left to its word family.

1. quick	mold unfold sold
2. marigold	plate gate crater
3. blame	mail pail rail
4. jump	goat throat coat
5. float	lump thump bumper
6. hesitate	frame game same
7. trail	flick thick pick

Did You Know?

Words in a word family often have the same set of letters that make a similar sound (the -ore in core, more, sore). If you can spell **dish**, you can spell **wish**!

16

B Say each sentence out loud. Underline the two words that are in the same word family. The first one is done for you.

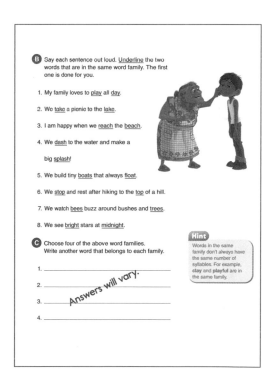

1. My family loves to <u>play</u> all <u>day</u>.

2. We <u>take</u> a picnic to the <u>lake</u>.

3. I am happy when we <u>reach</u> the <u>beach</u>.

4. We <u>dash</u> to the water and make a

   big <u>splash</u>!

5. We build tiny <u>boats</u> that always <u>float</u>.

6. We <u>stop</u> and rest after hiking to the <u>top</u> of a hill.

7. We watch <u>bees</u> buzz around bushes and <u>trees</u>.

8. We see <u>bright</u> stars at <u>midnight</u>.

C Choose four of the above word families. Write another word that belongs to each family.

1. _____

2. _____   *Answers will vary.*

3. _____

4. _____

Hint

Words in the same family don't always have the same number of syllables. For example, **clay** and **playful** are in the same family.

17

Sight and Sound

Mike and Sulley are practicing for the Scare Games. They need to look and sound scary!

Words aren't scary, but pay attention to how they look and sound.

A In each row, <u>underline</u> the words that are alike.

1.	<u>eight</u>	<u>freight</u>	trust	<u>weight</u>
2.	<u>truth</u>	peel	<u>booth</u>	<u>tooth</u>
3.	<u>mess</u>	Mike	<u>miss</u>	<u>moss</u>
4.	<u>puppy</u>	<u>purple</u>	pop	<u>puck</u>
5.	<u>try</u>	muddy	<u>cry</u>	<u>fry</u>
6.	<u>veil</u>	<u>mail</u>	ceiling	<u>male</u>

Did You Know?

Recognizing how words are alike can help you read new words. However, words may be alike in the way they look, but sound different (**tour** and **sour**). They can also be alike in the way they sound, but look different (**Sulley** and **Celia**, which both begin with the s sound).

18

B In each row, (circle) the letter or letters that make the same sound.

Hint
Say the words in each row and listen for similar sounds.

1. cl(ean)   m(ean)   b(ean)
2. m(en)   b(et)   th(em)
3. (sl)ip   (sl)eek   (sl)ide
4. sk(ate)   pl(ate)   d(ate)
5. cru(sh)   di(sh)   (sh)y
6. (ph)oto   (f)inal   (f)orm
7. ra(ng)   si(ng)   clu(ng)
8. m(oan)   gr(oan)   l(oan)
9. b(oo)   s(ou)p   t(oo)l
10. sc(are)   h(are)   m(are)

C Write five more words in the scare word family.

scare

Answers will vary.

19

Climb for New Words

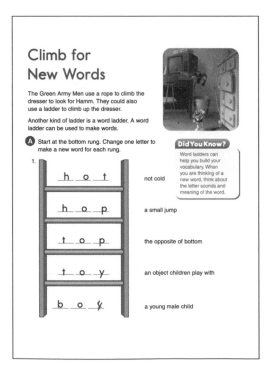

The Green Army Men use a rope to climb the dresser to look for Hamm. They could also use a ladder to climb up the dresser.

Another kind of ladder is a word ladder. A word ladder can be used to make words.

A Start at the bottom rung. Change one letter to make a new word for each rung.

Did You Know?
Word ladders can help you build your vocabulary. When you are thinking of a new word, think about the letter sounds and meaning of the word.

1.

h _ o _ t	not cold
h _ o _ p	a small jump
t _ o _ p	the opposite of bottom
t _ o _ y	an object children play with
b _ o _ y	a young male child

20

2.

t a k e	the opposite of give
t a p e	a sticky strip of material
t a l e	another word for a story
s a l e	an event when you can buy items cheaper
m a l e	a young or old man
m a n e	the hair on a horse's head
m i n e	belonging to me
d i n e	when you eat a meal
d i v e	to jump headfirst into the water

21

-Er, -Ar, -Or?

Miguel wants to be a guitar player. He meets Héctor in the Land of the Dead. Héctor asks for a favor. He wants his photo on Miguel's family altar.

Notice that **player**, **favor**, and **altar** all have a similar er sound.

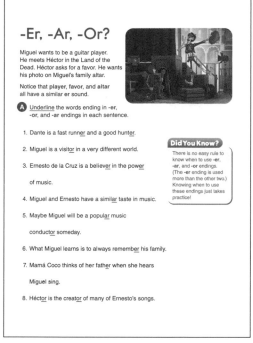

A Underline the words ending in -er, -or, and -ar endings in each sentence.

1. Dante is a fast runner and a good hunter.

2. Miguel is a visitor in a very different world.

3. Ernesto de la Cruz is a believer in the power

   of music.

4. Miguel and Ernesto have a similar taste in music.

5. Maybe Miguel will be a popular music

   conductor someday.

6. What Miguel learns is to always remember his family.

7. Mamá Coco thinks of her father when she hears

   Miguel sing.

8. Héctor is the creator of many of Ernesto's songs.

Did You Know?

There is no easy rule to know when to use -er, -ar, and -or endings. (The -er ending is used more than the other two.) Knowing when to use these endings just takes practice!

22

B Add an -er, -ar, or -or to complete the word in each sentence.

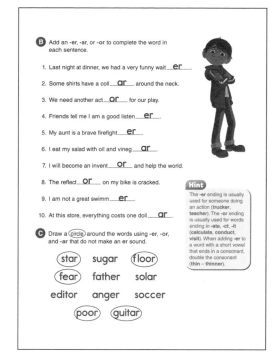

1. Last night at dinner, we had a very funny wait__er__.

2. Some shirts have a coll__ar__ around the neck.

3. We need another act__or__ for our play.

4. Friends tell me I am a good listen__er__.

5. My aunt is a brave firefight__er__.

6. I eat my salad with oil and vineg__ar__.

7. I will become an invent__or__ and help the world.

8. The reflect__or__ on my bike is cracked.

9. I am not a great swimm__er__.

10. At this store, everything costs one doll__ar__.

C Draw a circle around the words using -er, -or, and -ar that do not make an er sound.

(star)   sugar   (floor)

(fear)   father   solar

editor   anger   soccer

(poor)   (guitar)

Hint

The -er ending is usually used for someone doing an action (**trucker, teacher**). The -or ending is usually used for words ending in -ate, -ct, -it (**calculate, conduct, visit**). When adding -er to a word with a short vowel that ends in a consonant, double the consonant (**thin – thinner**).

23

Grrr-eat Base Words

Bo helps Woody find Forky. You could call her helpful.

Help is the **base word** of helpful.

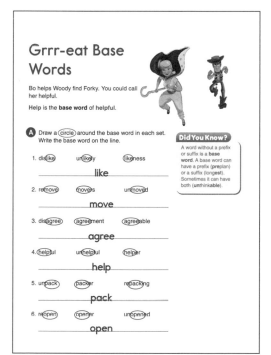

A Draw a circle around the base word in each set. Write the base word on the line.

1. dis(like)   un(like)ly   (like)ness

   _____like_____

2. re(move)   (move)rs   un(move)d

   _____move_____

3. dis(agree)   (agree)ment   (agree)able

   _____agree_____

4. (help)ful   un(help)ful   (help)er

   _____help_____

5. un(pack)   (pack)er   re(pack)ing

   _____pack_____

6. re(open)   (open)er   un(open)ed

   _____open_____

Did You Know?

A word without a prefix or suffix is a **base word**. A base word can have a prefix (**pre**plan) or a suffix (long**est**). Sometimes it can have both (**un**think**able**).

24

B Find the word in each sentence that has a prefix or a suffix. Underline the base word within that word.

Hint

A base word must be a complete word on its own. But, sometimes a letter is dropped when a suffix is added (**smile – smiling**).

1. Rex's roar could be stronger.

2. He is scared of frightful things.

3. He speaks nervously when he is afraid.

4. He is often hiding under things.

5. His friends don't like to hurt his feelings.

6. They treat him with kindness.

7. Woody came to untangle Rex.

8. Rex is hardly ever unhappy.

C Follow the instructions to invent new words! Define your words.

1. Add a suffix to a base word. _____

   Definition: _____

2. Add a prefix to a base word. _____

   Definition: _____

   Answers will vary.

3. Add a prefix and a suffix to a base word. _____

   Definition: _____

25

Preview Prefixes

Cruz Ramirez and Lightning McQueen do a lot of prerace work.

Pre- is a prefix that means "before." Prerace means "before the race."

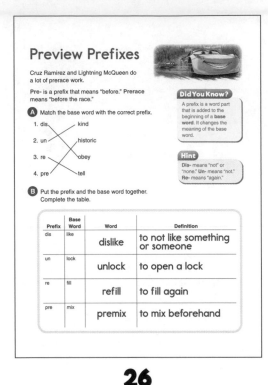

Did You Know?

A prefix is a word part that is added to the beginning of a **base word**. It changes the meaning of the base word.

A Match the base word with the correct prefix.

1. dis   kind
2. un   historic
3. re   obey
4. pre   tell

Hint

Dis- means "not" or "none." Un- means "not." Re- means "again."

B Put the prefix and the base word together. Complete the table.

Prefix	Base Word	Word	Definition
dis	like	dislike	to not like something or someone
un	lock	unlock	to open a lock
re	fill	refill	to fill again
pre	mix	premix	to mix beforehand

26

C Choose the correct prefix to complete the word.

dis-   un-   re-   pre-

1. After stalling, Lightning has to __re__ start his engine.
2. Lightning and Cruz practice hard in the __pre__ season.
3. Trainers and racers sometimes __dis__ agree about how to get ready for a race.
4. Lightning is __un__ happy about arguing with Cruz.
5. Cruz's worries __dis__ appear when she hits the track.

D Choose three of the words you completed in Part A, B, or C. Use each in a sentence.

_____

__Answers will vary.__

_____

_____

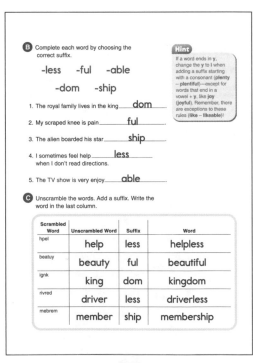

27

How Does It End?

At Monsters University, Sulley makes Mike feel good by telling him that he is fearless.

Fearless is a word that uses the suffix -less.

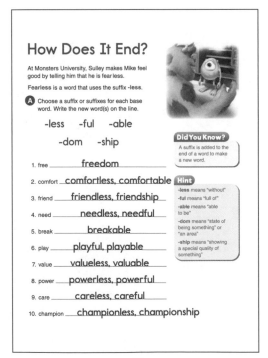

A Choose a suffix or suffixes for each base word. Write the new word(s) on the line.

-less   -ful   -able

-dom   -ship

Did You Know?

A suffix is added to the end of a word to make a new word.

1. free ___ **freedom**
2. comfort ___ **comfortless, comfortable**
3. friend ___ **friendless, friendship**
4. need ___ **needless, needful**
5. break ___ **breakable**
6. play ___ **playful, playable**
7. value ___ **valueless, valuable**
8. power ___ **powerless, powerful**
9. care ___ **careless, careful**
10. champion ___ **championless, championship**

Hint

-less means "without"
-ful means "full of"
-able means "able to be"
-dom means "state of being something" or "an area"
-ship means "showing a special quality of something"

28

B Complete each word by choosing the correct suffix.

-less   -ful   -able

-dom   -ship

1. The royal family lives in the king __dom__
2. My scraped knee is pain __ful__
3. The alien boarded his star __ship__
4. I sometimes feel help __less__ when I don't read directions.
5. The TV show is very enjoy __able__

Hint

If a word ends in y, change the y to i when adding a suffix starting with a consonant (plenty – plentiful)—except for words that end in a vowel + y, like joy (joyful). Remember, there are exceptions to these rules (like – likeable)!

C Unscramble the words. Add a suffix. Write the word in the last column.

Scrambled Word	Unscrambled Word	Suffix	Word
hpel	help	less	helpless
beatuy	beauty	ful	beautiful
ignk	king	dom	kingdom
rivred	driver	less	driverless
mebrem	member	ship	membership

29

A Nice, Pleasant, Good, Fine Dog

Dante is a good friend to Miguel. Dante is a pal, a buddy, a companion, a chum.

The words in purple are all **synonyms** for the word **friend**.

A Match each word to its synonym.

1. teach   difficult
2. journey   instruct
3. challenging   trip
4. brief   like
5. pleased   short
6. enjoy   satisfied

30

B Replace the **purple** word in each sentence with one of the listed synonyms.

races   unhappy

achieve   wonder

1. When Miguel feels **down**, he plays his guitar.

u	n	h	a	p	p	y

2. Ernesto de la Cruz tells Miguel to **reach** for his dreams.

a	c	h	i	e	v	e

3. Dante **dashes** through the streets.

r	a	c	e	s

4. Miguel is filled with **awe**.

w	o	n	d	e	r

> **Hint**
> Use a thesaurus to help you find synonyms.

C Write two synonyms for each word.

1. tiny _____

2. say _____

Answers will vary.

31

Yes and No, High and Low

Mike and Sulley are opposites. Mike is small while Sulley is big. Mike is studious while Sulley is carefree. Mike's roar is quiet. Sulley's roar is loud!

Words have opposites, or **antonyms**, too.

A Draw a (circle) around the antonym in each group of words.

1. wrong   (right)   incorrect
2. (indoors)   outdoors   outside
3. (easy)   hard   difficult
4. healthy   (sick)   well
5. wide   thick   (narrow)
6. same   (different) alike

B Write a sentence using the antonym of each word.

1. dry

_____

2. cheerful

Answers will vary.

32

C Complete the puzzle with antonyms for the listed words.

1. T A L L
2. F R I E N D L Y
3. E X C I T I N G
4. O V E R
5. C O N F I D E N T
6. S U N N Y
7. M A N Y
8. A S L E E P

1. short   2. unfriendly
3. boring   4. under
5. nervous   6. rainy
7. few   8. awake

33

Two for One

It's a special day at the speedway!

Speedway is a compound word.

A Place a check mark beside the cars that have compound words in their name.

✓ Chuck Armstrong	✓ Darrell Cartrip
✓ Kevin Racingtire	___ Sally Carrera
✓ Billy Oilchanger	___ River Scott
✓ Kevin Shiftright	___ Junior Moon
___ Cal Weathers	___ Shannon Spokes
✓ Arvy Motorhome	✓ Brent Mustangburger
✓ Bubba Wheelhouse	✓ Darren Leadfoot

> **Did You Know?**
> The meaning of a **compound word** is often related to both words (**hailstorm, toothpaste, cupcake**).

B Draw a (circle) around the compound words.

Put a slash between the two words that make the compound.

race/track   cheering   speeding

performance   head/light   along/side

compete   zoomed   week/end

thunderous   grand/stand   retirement

34

C These compound words got mixed up. Fix them!

poptub   lightcorn   suitbulb

bathnail   passcase   fingerword

1. pop + **corn** = **popcorn**
2. light + **bulb** = **lightbulb**
3. suit + **case** = **suitcase**
4. bath + **tub** = **bathtub**
5. pass + **word** = **password**
6. finger + **nail** = **fingernail**

D Create compound names for three cars.

1. _____
2. ___ *Answers will vary.*
3. _____

35

We're All for Contractions!

Sometimes, things can be turned into something else. Bonnie took trash and turned it into Forky! Make contractions by turning two words into one.

A Write the contraction made from the two words.

1. is not **isn't**
2. have not **haven't**
3. I am **I'm**
4. you are **you're**
5. did not **didn't**
6. would not **wouldn't**

> **Did You Know?**
> A **contraction** is a combination of two shortened words. An apostrophe takes the place of the missing letter(s).

B Write the two words that make up the contraction.

1. we're **we are**
2. she's **she is**
3. shouldn't **should not**
4. there's **there is**
5. he's **he is**

36

C Draw a (circle) around the correct contraction.

1. What is another way to say **it is**?
   (it's)   mightha've   mightv'e

2. What is another way to say **they will**?
   (they'll)   the'll   theyi'll

3. What is another way to say **that is**?
   thats   (that's)   tha'ts

4. What is another way to say **are not**?
   (aren't)   are'nt   aren'ot

5. What is another way to say **you are**?
   your   your'e   (you're)

6. What is another way to say **they have**?
   theyh've   (they've)   theyv'e

7. What is another way to say **she will**?
   (she'll)   shei'll   she'ill

D Write a sentence that has two contractions.

_____
___ *Answers will vary.*
_____

37

Short and Sweet

Sulley and Mike go to Monsters University (MU). After they graduate, they hope to work at Monsters, Incorporated (Monsters, Inc.).

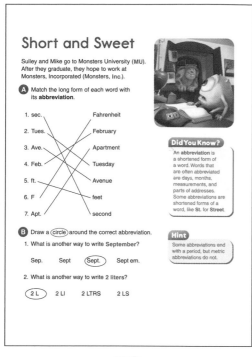

A Match the long form of each word with its **abbreviation**.

1. sec.	Fahrenheit
2. Tues.	February
3. Ave.	Apartment
4. Feb.	Tuesday
5. ft.	Avenue
6. F	feet
7. Apt.	second

Did You Know?

An **abbreviation** is a shortened form of a word. Words that are often abbreviated are days, months, measurements, and parts of addresses. Some abbreviations are shortened forms of a word, like **St.** for **Street**.

B Draw a circle around the correct abbreviation.

1. What is another way to write September?

Sep.   Sept   (Sept.)   Sept em.

2. What is another way to write 2 liters?

(2 L)   2 LI   2 LTRS   2 LS

Hint

Some abbreviations end with a period, but metric abbreviations do not.

38

---

3. What is another way to write Highway 10?

Hiw 10   (Hwy. 10)   hwy. 10   Hiway 10

4. What is another way to write Wednesday?

wed   Wednes.   Wen.   (Wed.)

C Fill in the chart.

Word(s)	Abbreviations
Friday, March 30	Fri., Mar. 30
Professor	Prof.
20 seconds	20 sec.
Oozma Kappa	OK
Thursday	Thurs.
3 feet	3 ft.
Sunday, April 1	Sun., Apr. 1

39

Spelling Strategies

Miguel loves to play guitar.

Guitar is a tricky word to spell. You can use rhymes and other memory prompts to help you spell tricky words.

A Read the spelling rules. Write the complete words in the third column. The first one is done for you.

Rule	Rule in Use	Final Words
u after q	squ + ad / qu + een	squad / queen
when a word ends in a consonant + y, change y to i when adding an ending, unless the ending is -ing	supply + ing / happy + er	supplying / happier
if adding an ending that starts with a vowel, drop silent e and throw in the towel	race + er / trace + ing	racer / tracing
short vowel, consonant, plus a vowel ending—double up the consonant, because it needs some friending	hop + er / drop + ing	hopper / dropping

Did You Know?

There are sometimes exceptions to spelling rules. For example, if a short vowel is followed by the letter x, the x is not doubled (**fix – fixed**).

40

B Follow the rules in Part A to spell each of these words correctly.

1. Add -est to funny. ____ funniest
2. Spell the opposite of loud. ____ quiet
3. Add -er to shop. ____ shopper
4. Add -ous to fame. ____ famous
5. Spell the sound that ducks make. ____ quack
6. Add -ing to win. ____ winning

C Correct the spelling mistake in each purple word.

1. The daiseys in the vase are wilting. ____ daisies
2. Are the cookies bakeing? ____ baking
3. Your qestions are important. ____ questions
4. The rabbits are hoping all around the yard. ____ hopping
5. To make the cake batter, we mixxed the sugar and butter first. ____ mixed
6. We saw many cars raceing around the track. ____ racing
7. She is happyest when her dog is at home. ____ happiest
8. The qeust to find library books was successful. ____ quest

41

Cruise by the Pit Crews

Let's hope Lightning McQueen's **brake** pedal doesn't **break**!

The words **brake** and **break** are examples of **homophones**.

A Read each word. Listen to how it sounds. Write a homophone for each word.

1. mail __male__
2. plain __plane__
3. blue __blew__
4. aunt __ant__
5. where __wear__
6. cheep __cheap__
7. cell __sell__
8. rap __wrap__
9. waist __waste__
10. eye __I__

Did You Know?
Homophones are words that sound the same but have different spellings and meanings, like **brake** and **break**.

B Draw a (circle) around the correct homophone in each sentence.

1. Lightning and Cruz Ramirez practice on a sandy (beach) beech.
2. The racers drove threw (through) the woods.
3. Sometimes racers skid write (right) into tires.
4. Races are sometimes held at knight (night.)
5. Lightning sometimes flies passed (past) Cruz.
6. In another race, Cruz easily (beats) beets Lightning.
7. On the dirt track, the tires scent (sent) mud flying.
8. Racers love to say, "I one (won!")

C Write two homophones for each word.

1. bye __buy__ __by__
2. sow __so__ __sew__
3. too __to__ __two__

Hint
Try inventing ways to remember which spelling to use. For example, you see with two eyes, so "two ee's for two eyes." Or, to remember the difference between **their** and **there**, think of the word **where**. **Where** means a place, which has a similar spelling to the word **there**, also a place.

It's Raining Cats and Dogs

Whoa! Sometimes the toys **get in hot water**.

This **idiom** means they get into trouble.

A Use your eagle eye to match the idiom to the correct meaning.

1. a green thumb — good at gardening
2. a piece of cake — very easy
3. get a kick out of — really enjoy
4. read between the lines — infer, or use clues
5. the apple of my eye — the thing I love most
6. let the cat out of the bag — tell a secret
7. gets my goat — is annoying
8. hold your horses — wait
9. go out on a limb — make a risky choice
10. get all your ducks in a row — plan

Did You Know?
An **idiom** is an expression that doesn't really mean what the words say. Idioms are a type of figurative language. They add interest and energy when you speak or write.

B Underline the idiom in each sentence. Write its meaning in the second column.

Idiom	Meaning
1. The toys wait on pins and needles for Bonnie to play with them.	anxiously
2. Some toys are on the fence about Forky being one of them.	undecided
3. Bo keeps her chin up when she is facing hard times.	stays positive
4. Forky feels like a fish out of water when he's not in the trash.	in a strange situation
5. Woody and Forky are in the same boat when they get lost.	in the same situation
6. Woody getting lost was a blessing in disguise.	something that seems bad or unlucky at first, but results in something good happening later
7. Bo was over the moon that Woody decided to stay with her.	very happy

C Make up your own idiom! Explain what your idiom means. Use it in a sentence.

Idiom: _____

Meaning: _____
Answers will vary.

Sentence: _____

Page 51

Mamá Imelda demands to know why she can't cross into the Land of the Living. Suddenly, out of the corner of her eye, she sees her family and a young boy walking toward her. She recognizes the young boy as her living great-great-grandson Miguel. He is holding an old photo. As they get closer, she can see the familiar faces of a woman and a young girl in the photo Miguel is holding.

"I think I know what happened," Mamá Imelda says crossly.

Hint

To make inferences, ask yourself questions like these: Why is this information here? What do these words tell me? What do the character's words and actions tell me?

B Answer the questions. Explain which clues helped you make this inference.

1. Are many people leaving the Land of the Dead?

   Many people are leaving the Land of the Dead because Mamá Imelda has to stand in a very long line at the station.

2. Did Mamá Imelda's family forget to put her photo on the *ofrenda*?

   Mamá Imelda's photo is not on the ofrenda because Miguel has it. This can be inferred from Mamá Imelda's familiarity with the photo he is holding.

51

Page 54

Who's in the Driver's Seat?

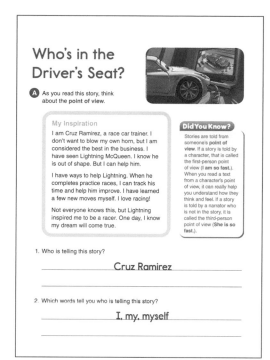

A As you read this story, think about the **point of view**.

My Inspiration

I am Cruz Ramirez, a race car trainer. I don't want to blow my own horn, but I am considered the best in the business. I have seen Lightning McQueen. I know he is out of shape. But I can help him.

I have ways to help Lightning. When he completes practice races, I can track his time and help him improve. I have learned a few new moves myself. I love racing!

Not everyone knows this, but Lightning inspired me to be a racer. One day, I know my dream will come true.

Did You Know?

Stories are told from someone's **point of view**. If a story is told by a character, that is called the first-person point of view (**I am so fast.**). When you read a text from a character's point of view, it can really help you understand how they think and feel. If a story is told by a narrator who is not in the story, it is called the third-person point of view (**She is so fast.**).

1. Who is telling this story?

   Cruz Ramirez

2. Which words tell you who is telling this story?

   I, my, myself

54

Page 55

3. Is the story written from a first-person point of view or a third-person point of view? How do you know?

   first-person point of view; I know because it is being told from Cruz Ramirez's point of view.

B Rewrite Cruz's story from Lightning's point of view. The first two sentences are written for you.

   My name is Lightning McQueen. I'm a very famous race car!

   Answers will vary.

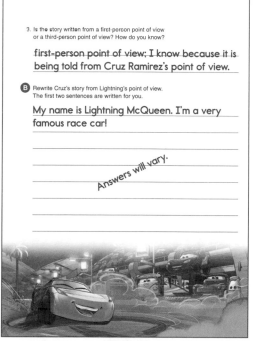

55

Page 56

Getting the Message

Some monsters and Boo are in a restaurant. Suddenly, the monsters realize Boo is there. All of the monsters panic and try to get away from Boo. A table is knocked over. Trays and food are flying.

A Draw a (circle) around the **main idea**.

Did You Know?

The **main idea** tells us what the text is about. To find the main idea, separate the most important idea from the less important details.

   Monsters like to eat in restaurants.

   (The monsters are afraid of Boo.)

   Boo eats food.

   Trays and food are flying.

56

B As you read this journal entry, think about its main idea.

October 16

Today in class, we wrote about what it takes to be a good customer at a restaurant. The most important part of being a good customer is simple: just be polite.

The next time I go to a restaurant, I will make sure to chew my food quietly. I will not throw food or run around while people are eating. I will also treat the restaurant staff nicely. I shouldn't scream and turn over tables if I see something I don't like in the restaurant.

I can't wait to go to a restaurant and practice what I learned today about being a good customer.

Hint

To find the main idea, look for words that are repeated. Look for language that is strong and direct. Ask yourself: What do I think the author really wants me to remember?

1. What is the main idea in this journal entry?

   The main idea is to be polite when you are a customer in a restaurant.

2. What helped you identify the main idea?

   There are tips showing you how to be a good customer.

57

1. Title	Our Planet Earth
2. What is the subject of this article?	Earth has many special features.
3. Why did the author write this article?	The author wrote this article to show Earth's special features.
4. What are three important ideas from this article?	a) The average temperature on Earth is 57 degrees Fahrenheit. b) As far as we know, Earth is the only planet in our solar system that has liquid water on its surface all the time. c) Earth rotates around the Sun in 24 hours.
5. Summarize the article in two sentences.	Earth has many special features. Its average temperature is 57 degrees, it is the only planet with liquid water on its surface all of the time, and it only takes 24 hours to rotate around the Sun.

59

When All Is Said and Done

As Miguel leaves Ernesto de la Cruz's tomb, he runs straight home without stopping. He needs to make sure Mamá Coco remembers her father.

When he arrives home, Miguel asks Mamá Coco if she remembers her father. When she can't remember him, Miguel does not give up. He picks up his guitar and plays her father's song. Mamá Coco's face lights up and she starts singing along.

Did You Know?

You can **draw conclusions** using the available facts, or evidence, in the text. How you understand the evidence will help you make a decision about what you have just read.

A Use evidence in the text to answer these questions.

1. Do you think Miguel feels it is important that Mamá Coco remembers her father?

   Miguel feels it is really important that Mamá Coco remembers her father.

2. What evidence helps you draw your conclusion?

   This is shown by Miguel running home without stopping. He also does not give up after the first time he asks Mamá Coco to remember her father. He tries again.

60

The following year, as always, families prepare their *ofrendas* for *Día de los Muertos*. However, Ernesto de la Cruz's large tomb now looks very different than in previous years. News has spread about how he had poisoned Héctor Rivera. His tomb has a sign on it that says "Forget you."

The Rivera shoe shop also looks different. Tour groups now stop by the shop. The tour guide explains that this was the home of Héctor Rivera, the great songwriter.

B Draw conclusions, using evidence from the text.

1. What conclusion can you draw about Ernesto's reputation? Why do you think so?

   I conclude that Ernesto is not as popular anymore, because his tomb has a sign that says, "Forget you."

2. Do you think Ernesto deserves the reputation he has now? Why or why not?

   Answers will vary.

61

B Evaluate the text.

1. Summarize the text in one sentence.

Sid thinks museums are boring, crowded, and tiring.

2. What is the main idea?

Sid does not like museums.

3. Does the author support his ideas with facts? Explain.

Sid supports his ideas by explaining that museums are crowded and have exhibits that are not interesting. He prefers virtual tours instead. He does not support his ideas with facts, just opinions.

4. Do you agree with the author's main idea? Why or why not?

Answers will vary.

5. What questions do you have after reading the text?

Answers will vary.

63

A Complete the problem-and-solution graphic organizer for the story you have just read.

Problem

Lightning does not know what to do after a bad crash.

Hint
Words and phrases such as **problem, issue, challenge, one thing to do, another way, as a result,** and **the answer is,** are often hints that you are reading a problem-and-solution text.

Solution
Lightning can retire from racing.

Solution
Lightning can practice on equipment that Jackson Storm uses.

Solution
Lightning can train with Cruz Ramirez.

What Happens

Lightning agrees to train with Cruz.

65

A Use this graphic organizer to outline the story elements for the story you have just read.

Setting

Monsters, Inc., in Monstropolis

Characters

Sulley, Mike, Boo, Randall

Plot

Beginning
Mike and Sulley find a little girl named Boo.

Middle
They keep her safe from a monster named Randall.

End
Boo goes home.

B Summarize the story in one sentence.

Mike and Sulley rescue Boo, a little girl who has arrived in Monstropolis.

67

A Fill in the blank with the correct word for each text feature definition.

heading   title   list

paragraph   keyword

Did You Know?
Text features help you know what kind of text you are going to read, like a magazine article or a nonfiction book. Text features help you see how the information is organized.

1. the name of the text

title

2. a group of sentences that all have to do with the same idea

paragraph

3. the name of a section of text; it tells what that section is about

heading

4. a word in bold type to show that the text includes a definition for the word, usually in the margin or at the end

keyword

5. items set in a text one under the other; often start with a bullet, dash, or number

list

B Read "About Guitars" again. Underline its text features. Then, label the text features.

69

Panel 71

A Draw a (circle) around the correct **purple** word.
Fill in the blanks with an example from the dog bathing instructions.

1. Instructions are written in the (present) past tense.

   Example: _____

   Answers will vary.

2. Instructions (tell) ask readers what to do.

   Example: _____

   Answers will vary.

3. Instructions are presented in (order) random order.

   Example: _____

   Answers will vary.

4. Instructions may have a list of (materials) characters.

   Example: _____

   Answers will vary.

5. Instructions are very confusing (clear.)

   Example: _____

   Answers will vary.

71

Panel 72

Seeing Is Believing

Natalie Certain knows the racing statistics of all the racers at the Piston Cup. She can use a table to organize and compare all of her statistics.

A Read the table. Then, answer the questions.

Car Details

Racer	Performance	Body Material
Lightning McQueen	• 0–60 mi in 4 seconds • top speed is 198 mi/h	• cold-rolled sheet metal
Cruz Ramirez	• 0–60 mi in 3.8 seconds • top speed is 210 mi/h	• lightweight alloy
Jackson Storm	• 0–60 mi in 3.6 seconds • top speed is 214 mi/h	• coated carbon fiber and metal composite

1. Who has the fastest top speed?

   Jackson Storm

2. What material is Lightning's body made of?

   cold-rolled sheet metal

3. How long does it take for Cruz to go from 0 mi to 60 mi?

   3.8 seconds

4. Explain how you got your answers from the table.

   Answers will vary.

72

Panel 73

B Examine the diagram of Mack. Answer the questions.

Mack's Parts

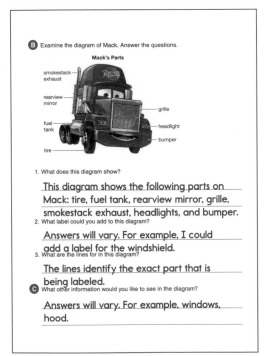

smokestack exhaust

rearview mirror

fuel tank

tire

grille

headlight

bumper

1. What does this diagram show?

   This diagram shows the following parts on Mack: tire, fuel tank, rearview mirror, grille, smokestack exhaust, headlights, and bumper.

2. What label could you add to this diagram?

   Answers will vary. For example, I could add a label for the windshield.

3. What are the lines for in this diagram?

   The lines identify the exact part that is being labeled.

C What other information would you like to see in the diagram?

   Answers will vary. For example, windows, hood.

73

Panel 74

Let's Talk!

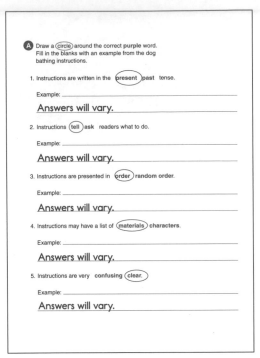

Mike and Sulley pull off an impressive scare at a camp. A reporter from the Monsters University student newspaper, *The Campus Roar*, interviews them.

title

An Interview with Heroes

Students Mike Wazowski (MW) and James P. Sullivan (JS) pulled off a legendary scare. They tell The Campus Roar (TCR) what happened. → introduction

TCR: What happened the day of the scare? → question

MW: I wanted to prove to everyone I was a good Scarer, so I decided to scare a kid by myself. → answer

TCR: Can you tell us about where the scare happened?

MW: I walked through a door into the human world. I first thought I was in a child's bedroom, but it turned out I was in an entire cabin of campers! → names of people speaking

TCR: Sulley, how were you feeling knowing that Mike was in the human world by himself?

JS: I was really worried about him.

TCR: What did you do?

JS: I decided to go in after him, even though Dean Hardscrabble told me it was really dangerous.

TCR: That's a great ending! Thank you for talking to us today. → ending

74

Care to Join Us?

Miguel crosses a bridge that joins two worlds.

In language, there are words that act like bridges. They are called **conjunctions**.

A Complete each sentence with one of these conjunctions: **and, but,** or **so.**

1. Dante is hungry, **so** Miguel feeds him.

2. Miguel **and** Mamá Coco enjoy being together.

3. Miguel loves music, **but** Abuelita does not allow him to play it.

B Choose the best conjunction for each sentence.

and   but   so

1. I put on my raincoat **and** dashed to the bus.

2. You look bored, **so** let's play a game.

3. They feel happy **and** excited.

4. I am allergic to peanuts, **but** not to other nuts.

5. My bike tire is flat, **so** I need to fix it.

6. I would love to have a horse, **but** we don't have a barn.

7. She loves both swimming **and** diving.

8. He can't reach the top shelf, **so** he uses a step stool.

> **Hint**
> Try each conjunction in each sentence. The right one will show the relationship between the two parts being joined.

C Write a sentence for each conjunction: **and, but,** and **so.**

1. _____
2. _____ *Answers will vary.*
3. _____

D Write a sentence that uses two conjunctions.

_____ *Answers will vary.*

82

83

Can-Do Commas

Miguel lives in Santa Cecilia, Mexico. He is excited for *Día de los Muertos.* The celebration begins October 31.

Miguel knows a comma is needed between the names of cities and states and cities and countries. He also knows a comma is needed between the day and the year when writing a date.

A Add a comma where it is needed in the dates and places below.

1. Mexico City, Mexico

2. June 6, 2020

3. Las Cruces, New Mexico

4. September 9, 2016

5. Amarillo, Texas

6. January 20, 2000

7. Puebla, Mexico

84

First, Read This

First, Bonnie is scared to go to school. **Next,** Woody sneaks in her backpack to watch over her. **Then,** they both go to school. **Soon,** Bonnie makes Forky. **Finally,** she starts to feel better about school!

A Number the sentences in the order the events take place. The **sequence words** can help you.

7 Finally, I went to bed, where I would be safe!

4 Next, I arrived at school, but I tripped on the stairs. Ouch again!

3 Soon, I recovered and made my way to school.

5 I managed to get through the rest of the day unharmed.

2 Then, while eating breakfast, I got grapefruit juice in my eye!

6 Later that evening, my sister accidentally whacked my thumb.

1 First, I tripped on my bedroom rug and fell—ouch!

> **Did You Know?**
> **Sequence words** help you put events in the order in which they happen. Some other sequence words are **first, then, second, before, after, while, during.** They don't always have to start the sentence, and they don't have to be used in every sentence.

> **Hint**
> Visualize the action and settings to help you put the events in the right order.

86

B Add sequence words to this paragraph.

first   next   then

soon   later   finally

Hint
Some blanks have more than one right answer.

_____First_____, we unpack the car.

_____Next_____, we set up our tent

and stove. _____Soon_____, we begin

cooking our dinner. _____Then_____,

we play for a while. _____Later_____,

we make a fire. _____Finally_____, we

head to bed!

C Write a short paragraph about something you did recently. Use at least four sequence words.

Answers will vary.

87

Fuzzy, Fuzzier, Fuzziest

The Oozma Kappa team uses **comparing adjectives** to describe each other: Art is the fuzziest member of the team. Sulley is the tallest. Don is short, but Mike and Squishy are shorter.

You can use comparing adjectives to describe things in your life, too.

A Complete the table by filling in the missing words.

Adjective	Adjective with -er	Adjective with -est
loud	louder	loudest
sad	sadder	saddest
happy	happier	happiest
funny	funnier	funniest
young	younger	youngest
bright	brighter	brightest

Did You Know?
Comparing adjectives are used to compare two or more nouns. To make most comparing adjectives, just add the suffix **-er** or **-est**. For two-syllable adjectives ending in a consonant + **y**, like **fuzzy**, change the **y** to **i** and add the suffix. For words that are a consonant-vowel-consonant, like **big**, double the final consonant (**biggest**).

88

B Read each sentence. Complete the sentence with the correct form of the purple adjective.

1. That was the _____strongest_____ wind I have ever felt. **strong**

Hint
The adjectives that end in -est have the in front of them (**the biggest slice**).

2. My red shirt is _____warmer_____ than my blue one. **warm**

3. This hike will be _____tougher_____ than our last one. **tough**

4. The _____hardest_____ part about visiting Grandpa is saying goodbye. **hard**

5. My cousin tells the _____silliest_____ jokes you can imagine. **silly**

6. This way is _____quicker_____ than that way. **quick**

C Write a sentence using a comparing adjective of your choice. It can have an -er or -est ending.

Answers will vary.

89

Use Adverbs Happily!

Lightning McQueen tries anxiously to get away from Miss Fritter at the Thunder Hollow Speedway demolition derby. Other cars are spinning out uncontrollably. Mud flies everywhere.

The words anxiously, uncontrollably, and everywhere are **adverbs**.

A Underline the adverb in each sentence. Circle the verb described by the adverb.

1. The demolition derby is held weekly.

2. The cars confidently enter the racetrack.

3. The cars drive quickly.

4. All the engines roar noisily.

5. The cars navigate around obstacles.

6. Cars frequently crash into the obstacles.

7. Cruz Ramirez bravely enters the race.

8. New racers are sometimes welcomed rudely.

9. Cruz happily finishes in first place.

10. The crowd cheers wildly!

Did You Know?
An **adverb** is a word that describes a verb. It tells how, where, or when an action is done. Many adverbs are adjectives with the ending **-ly** added, (**safe – safely, kind – kindly**).

Hint
An adverb can go before or after the verb, but it stays close to the verb, without many other words between.

90

B Turn each purple word into an adverb.

1. I eat my ice cream _____slowly_____ . slow

2. He trudges _____tiredly_____ . tired

3. They _____awkwardly_____ lift the heavy box. awkward

4. The wolf licked its lips _____hungrily_____ hungry

5. _____Carefully_____ , I add an egg to the batter. careful

6. I email my grandparents _____monthly_____ month

7. She _____thoughtfully_____ held the door for everyone. thoughtful

8. The town _____wisely_____ planted trees at the dog park. wise

C Write two sentences that use adverbs. Underline the verbs described by the adverbs.

1. _____
_____
2. _____Answers will vary._____

91

Who Owns What?

Miguel shares his secret with Dante. The secret is theirs.

Without **possessive adjectives** and pronouns, we would not know who the secret belonged to.

A Draw a (circle) around the correct possessive adjective in each sentence.

1. I am proud of (my) me effort this year.

2. All the birds have flown from its (their) nests.

3. We should practice (our) her presentation.

4. Ellie forgot me (her) lunch again.

5. The cat cleans (its) their whiskers.

6. You and Amar can clean up you (your) toys now.

Did You Know?
A possessive adjective (my, your, her, his, its, our, their) describes the noun that follows it. It shows who or what the noun belongs to.
A possessive pronoun (mine, yours, his, hers, ours, yours, theirs) takes the place of a noun.

B Write a sentence for each of the possessive adjectives.

our   your   their

1. _____
2. _____
3. _____Answers will vary._____

92

C Fill in the blank with the correct possessive pronoun.

mine   his   hers   ours   yours   theirs

1. Ernesto de la Cruz got many gifts from his fans.

The gifts are _____his_____ .

2. The Los Chachalacos band has a sousaphone.

The sousaphone is _____theirs_____ .

3. The photo belongs to Mamá Imelda. It is _____hers_____

4. That is my guitar. That guitar is _____mine_____

5. You have a chance to perform. The chance to

perform is _____yours_____

6. This celebration belongs to my family and me.

This celebration is _____ours_____

D Write a sentence for each of the possessive pronouns.

yours   ours   theirs

1. _____
2. _____
3. _____Answers will vary._____

93

A (Circle) the correct plural noun for each word.

fox	cherry	dish
foxs	(cherries)	dishs
(foxes)	cherrys	(dishes)

couch	book	bus
(couches)	bookes	busies
couchs	(books)	(buses)

B (Circle) the correct plural noun for each word.

calf	man	mouse
(calves)	mens	moose
calvs	(men)	(mice)

person	foot	woman
(people)	feets	(women)
persons	(feet)	womans

95

Being Proper

The city of **Monstropolis** has a company called **Monsters, Inc.** Some monsters work there as **Scarers.**

The purple words above are **proper nouns.** Can you think of some other proper nouns?

A Underline each proper noun in these sentences.

1. Our neighbor, <u>Mrs. Kovac</u>, sometimes bakes

   for us.

2. One day I hope to visit <u>Cavendish Beach</u>.

3. We usually buy our vegetables at <u>Fresh

   Country Market</u>.

4. My oldest cousin is moving to <u>Australia</u>.

5. <u>Scooter</u> is the name of my friend's gerbil.

6. My favorite month is <u>May</u>.

Did You Know?

A **proper noun** names a specific person, place, or thing (**Emma, Canada, Wednesday**). Proper nouns are capitalized, even if they are not at the start of a sentence. **Common nouns** name general people, places, or things (**dancer, country, movie**) and do not need a capital letter, unless they appear at the beginning of a sentence.

96

B Correct the capitalization error(s) in each sentence.

1. We go to the dentist's office on tuesday.

   _____ Tuesday _____

2. My teacher's favorite Country is Iceland.

   _____ country _____

3. I belong to a club called ms. harvie's Dance World.

   _____ Ms. Harvie's _____

4. My younger Sister loves hockey.

   _____ sister _____

5. The title of my book is *danger marshmallows*.

   _____ *Danger Marshmallows* _____

C Answer each question with a proper noun.

1. Where do you live? _____

2. What is your full name? _____

3. What country would you like to visit? _____

4. What is a restaurant near you? _____

5. What is your favorite book or movie? _____

Answers will vary.

97

Abstract Activities

Mike felt great pride in his job at Monsters, Inc.

Pride is an **abstract noun.** Abstract nouns name feelings, concepts, and ideas. Some examples are childhood, wisdom, and hope.

A Underline the abstract noun or nouns in each sentence.

1. Sulley forms a <u>friendship</u> with Boo.

2. Sulley brings Boo great <u>joy</u>.

3. The citizens of Monstropolis feel <u>fear</u> when they see children.

4. Waternoose did not tell the <u>truth</u>.

5. Mike and Sulley rid Monstropolis of the <u>prejudice</u> against children.

6. They found that <u>laughter</u> could power Monstropolis.

98

B Fill in the blanks with an abstract noun from the box.

knowledge	courage	dream	hope

1. Mike's childhood _____ dream _____ was to be a Scarer.

2. Mike has a lot of _____ knowledge _____ about working at Monsters, Inc.

3. Sulley shows _____ courage _____ when he decides to help Boo.

4. Mike and Sulley have _____ hope _____ that they can make children laugh.

C Write three sentences of your own that use abstract nouns. Use the nouns from the exercises or think of your own.

1. _____

2. _____

3. _____

Answers will vary.

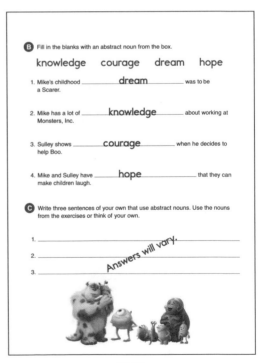

99

Making Sense of Tense

Ducky and Bunny play today. They played yesterday, too.

A Underline the verb in each sentence. Check the correct **verb tense**: past or present.

1. I <u>help</u> my dad with chores.

_____ past   ✓ present

2. Our bus <u>stops</u> at the railway crossing.

_____ past   ✓ present

3. We <u>planted</u> cucumbers in the spring.

✓ past   _____ present

4. The seagulls <u>screeched</u> overhead.

✓ past   _____ present

5. We <u>race</u> toward the swings.

_____ past   ✓ present

6. I <u>watched</u> the sunset last night.

✓ past   _____ present

Did You Know?

Verbs in the **present tense** describe an action that is happening right now. (I play soccer.) The **past tense** of a verb describes an action that has happened before. (I played soccer.) How did the verb **play** change when it became past tense? Not all past tense verbs use an -ed ending. Some verbs are irregular (the verb **buy** becomes **bought**; the verb **to be** becomes **was** or **were**).

100

B Write the past tense for these irregular verbs.

1. throw _____ **threw**
2. run _____ **ran**
3. say _____ **said**
4. eat _____ **ate**
5. see _____ **saw**
6. do _____ **did**

C Change each purple verb to the past tense.

1. I _____ **typed** _____ an email to my friend last night. type

2. They _____ **forgot** _____ to shut the gate again. forget

3. The kite _____ **flew** _____ well yesterday. flies

4. She _____ **scored** _____ the winning goal. scores

5. We _____ **made** _____ cupcakes for yesterday's bake sale. make

6. He _____ **lay** _____ down on the bed with his blanket. lie

Hint

For past-tense verbs ending in silent e, just add d (rake becomes raked).

101

Ready, Set, Action!

When Chick Hicks describes races, he uses a lot of precise **action verbs**. Instead of using the verb drive, he likes to say zoom, explode, fly, surge, or blaze instead. Action verbs help his descriptions sound more exciting!

A Change each purple verb to a more precise action verb. Cross out the first verb. The first one is done for you.

1. I ~~walk~~ _**stroll**_ to the park.

2. We speak _____ with the store manager.

3. She laughs _____ at the comedian's joke.

4. He sees _____ an eagle in the tree.

5. I take _____ the heavy box to the truck.

6. We eat _____ the delicious pizza.

7. He says _____ "Hey!" when he sees the bear.

8. I ran _____ home.

Answers will vary.

Did You Know?

Action verbs describe things that can be done. They also describe feelings and thoughts (enjoy, assume, think). Choosing precise action verbs helps your readers visualize exactly what you mean.

Hint

Use a thesaurus to help you expand your vocabulary and choose more precise action verbs.

102

B Solve each clue. Add the missing letters to complete the precise action verb.

1. to look very closely at something   e **X** a **m** ine

2. to run like a horse   g **a** l l **o p**

3. to speak very softly   **w** h **i s p** er

4. to shut a door loudly   **s** l **l** am

5. to drink something noisily   s **l** ur **p**

C Write a description of something exciting you have done or seen. Use precise action verbs.

Answers will vary.

_____

_____

_____

_____

_____

_____

_____

_____

103

Page 104

Quality Control

These employees at Monsters, Inc. check closely to catch any mistakes at the factory.

Writers need to check their work, too. After you have planned, written, and revised something, the next step is to edit it.

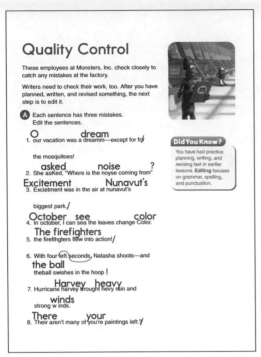

A Each sentence has three mistakes. Edit the sentences.

    O   dream
1. our vacation was a dreamm—except for for

    the mosquitoes!

    asked   noise
2. She asKed, "Where is the noyse coming from"

Excitement   Nunavut's
3. Excietment was in the air at nunavut's

    biggest park./

October   see   color
4. In october, I can sea the leaves change Color.

    The firefighters
5. the firefihgters flew into action!/

6. With four left seconds, Natasha shoots—and

the ball
theball swishes in the hoop !

    Harvey   heavy
7. Hurricane harvey brought hevy rain and

winds
strong w inds.

There   your
8. Their aren't many of you're paintings left./

> **Did You Know?**
> You have had practice planning, writing, and revising text in earlier lessons. **Editing** focuses on grammar, spelling, and punctuation.

Page 105

B An editing checklist can help you edit. Complete this checklist.

> **Editing Checklist**
> ☐ Are words spelled
>   ___correctly___ ?
> ☐ Does each sentence ___start___
>   with an uppercase letter?
> ☐ Does each sentence end with a
>   ___question mark___
>   period, _____, or
>   exclamation mark?
> ☐ Are sequence words in the right
>   ___order___ ?
> ☐ Are verbs in the correct
>   ___tense___ ?
> ☐ Are ___proper___ nouns
>   capitalized?

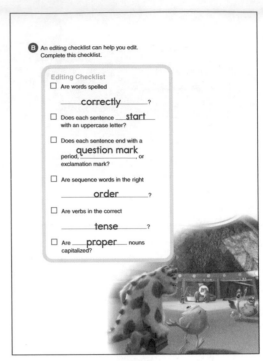

Page 106

Taking Numbers Apart

Hundreds of marigold petals swirl around Miguel as he plays Ernesto de la Cruz's guitar.

A Fill in the blanks to complete the expanded form of each number.

1. 745 __7__ hundreds + __4__ tens + __5__ ones

2. 220 __2__ hundreds + __2__ tens + __0__ ones

3. 108 __1__ hundreds + __0__ tens + __8__ ones

4. 576 __5__ hundreds + __7__ tens + __6__ ones

5. 621 __6__ hundreds + __2__ tens + __1__ ones

6. 79 __0__ hundreds + __7__ tens + __9__ ones

> **Did You Know?**
> Numbers can be written out in three ways: standard form (423), words (four hundred twenty-three), and expanded form (4 hundreds + 2 tens + 3 ones or 400 + 20 + 3).

B Write these numbers in words.

1. 739 __seven hundred thirty-nine__

2. 804 __eight hundred four__

3. 520 __five hundred twenty__

4. 213 __two hundred thirteen__

5. 107 __one hundred seven__

Page 107

C Complete the table.

Standard Form	Words	Expanded Form
462	four hundred sixty-two	400+60+2
696	six hundred ninety-six	600 + 90 + 6
91	ninety-one	90+1
348	three hundred forty-eight	300+40+8
952	nine hundred fifty-two	900 + 50 + 2
736	seven hundred thirty-six	700 + 30 + 6
501	five hundred one	500 + 1
17	seventeen	10+7
893	eight hundred ninety-three	800+90+3
48	forty-eight	40 + 8
111	one hundred eleven	100 + 10 + 1
288	two hundred eighty-eight	200+80+8
104	one hundred four	100+4

Get in Position!

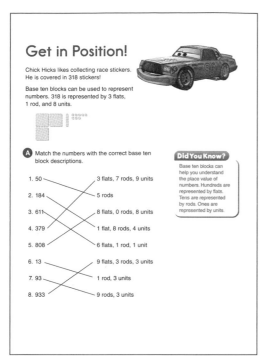

Chick Hicks likes collecting race stickers. He is covered in 318 stickers!

Base ten blocks can be used to represent numbers. 318 is represented by 3 flats, 1 rod, and 8 units.

A Match the numbers with the correct base ten block descriptions.

1. 50 — 3 flats, 7 rods, 9 units
2. 184 — 5 rods
3. 611 — 8 rods, 0 rods, 8 units
4. 379 — 1 flat, 8 rods, 4 units
5. 808 — 6 flats, 1 rod, 1 unit
6. 13 — 9 flats, 3 rods, 3 units
7. 93 — 1 rod, 3 units
8. 933 — 9 rods, 3 units

Did You Know?

Base ten blocks can help you understand the place value of numbers. Hundreds are represented by flats. Tens are represented by rods. Ones are represented by units.

B Draw base ten blocks to model each of the numbers. The first one is done for you.

Number	Hundreds	Tens	Ones
225	☐ ☐	‖	⁙
95		‖‖‖‖‖‖‖‖‖	⁙
432	☐ ☐ ☐ ☐	‖‖‖	▫▫

C Choose one of the above numbers and model the number a different way using base ten blocks.

Number	Hundreds	Tens	Ones
	Answers will vary.		

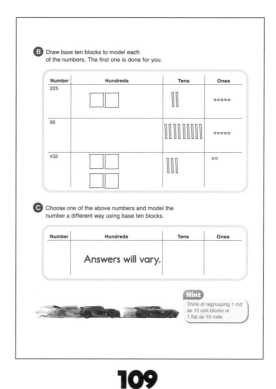

Hint

Think of regrouping 1 rod as 10 unit blocks or 1 flat as 10 rods.

I'm the Greatest!

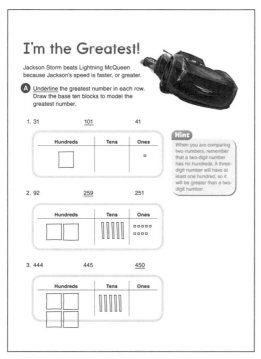

Jackson Storm beats Lightning McQueen because Jackson's speed is faster, or greater.

A Underline the greatest number in each row. Draw the base ten blocks to model the greatest number.

1. 31   <u>101</u>   41

Hundreds	Tens	Ones
☐		▫

Hint

When you are comparing two numbers, remember that a two-digit number has no hundreds. A three-digit number will have at least one hundred, so it will be greater than a two-digit number.

2. 92   <u>259</u>   251

Hundreds	Tens	Ones
☐ ☐	‖‖‖‖‖	▫▫▫▫▫ ▫▫▫▫

3. 444   445   <u>450</u>

Hundreds	Tens	Ones
☐ ☐ ☐ ☐	‖‖‖‖‖	

B Draw a (circle) around the greatest number in each set.

1. ninety	one hundred one	(one hundred ten)
2. nine hundred nine	(nine hundred ten)	nine hundred eight
3. (7 hundreds + 7 tens + 7 ones)	7 hundreds + 1 ten + 7 ones	7 hundreds + 0 tens + 7 ones
4. five hundred forty-two	four hundred twenty-nine	(six hundred seventy-three)
5. (5 hundreds + 2 tens + 1 one)	5 hundreds + 0 tens + 1 one	5 hundreds + 1 ten + 1 one

C Which car has the greatest average speed? Rank the cars from fastest to slowest.

Car	Average Speed	Ranking
Cruz Ramirez	2 hundreds + 7 ones mi/h	2
Jackson Storm	2 hundreds + 9 ones mi/h	1
Lightning McQueen	1 hundred + 8 tens + 15 ones mi/h	4
Chase Racelott	2 hundreds + 4 ones mi/h	3

Hint

Sometimes, tens can be represented by ones. For example, 64 can be represented by 6 tens and 4 ones. It can also be represented as 5 tens and 14 ones.

Smallest and Largest

As Miguel walks through the Land of the Dead, he sees many buildings. Some buildings in the Land of the Dead have many homes. Some buildings have just a few.

A Each number represents the amount of homes in a building. In each row, draw a (circle) around the smallest number. Underline the largest number.

1. (24)   702   554   87
2. 330   530   942   (120)
3. (98)   101   102   105
4. 202   208   210   (201)
5. (657)   756   675   765
6. 994   (94)   904   949

Did You Know?
When one number is smaller than another, we can show this using a **less than** sign (2 < 5). To show that one number is larger than another, we can use the **more than** sign (9 > 7).

B Write < or > to make each number statement true.

1. 101 ___>___ 98
2. 592 ___>___ 590
3. 608 ___<___ 680
4. 875 ___>___ 857
5. 253 ___>___ 235

C Write < or > to make each number statement true. Explain how you know.

1. 303 ___<___ 503

   Three hundreds is less than five hundreds.

2. 422 ___>___ 402

   Four hundreds is equal to four hundreds, but zero tens is less than two tens.

3. 750 ___>___ 650

   Six hundreds is less than seven hundreds.

D Determine which number statements are not true. Rewrite them correctly.

1. 555 < 505   incorrect 555 > 505
2. 98 < 105   correct
3. 471 < 417   incorrect 471 > 417
4. 17 > 117   incorrect 17 < 117

What's the Order?

Sulley and Mike have scare practice every night. Their scaring is getting really good!

A Organize the number of times they scare from least to greatest.

1. 385   212   198   387   306

   198, 212, 306, 385, 387

2. 785   796   801   800   797

   785, 796, 797, 800, 801

3. 164   99   97   500   275

   97, 99, 164, 275, 500

Hint
Working from left to right can help you order numbers. Start by comparing the hundreds value. Then, compare the tens value, and then compare the ones value.

4. 751   75   750   570   57

   57, 75, 570, 750, 751

5. 66   6   660   606   661

   6, 66, 606, 660, 661

6. 991   499   389   950   999

   389, 499, 950, 991, 999

B Which numbers can you make using the digits 1 5 3?

1. Make the largest number possible. __531__
2. Make the smallest number possible. __135__

Hint
The smallest number will have the least hundreds. The greatest number will have the most hundreds.

3. Write four more numbers that you can make using the digits 1 5 3.

   315   351   513   153

4. Order all the numbers that you made from least to greatest.

   135 , 153 , 315 , 351 , 513 , 531

C Sulley and Mike count the number of scare cans in the door tech lab every day for one week.

590   293   887   878   367   356   778

1. Write the numbers in order from least to greatest.

   293, 356, 367, 590, 778, 878, 887

2. Explain how you knew in which order to put the numbers.

   Answers will vary. For example, look at the hundreds values and then the tens values and ones values to put the numbers in order.

Rounding the Curve

Cruz Ramirez wears number 51. You can round her number to the nearest ten, which is 50.

A Use the number line to help you round to the nearest ten as you answer each question.

←—|—|—|—|—|—|—|—|—|—|—|—|—|—|—|—|→
60 62 64 66 68 70 72 74 76 78 80 82 84 86 88 90

1. Find 61 on the number line. Which tens value is it closer to, 60 or 70?

   60

2. Find 86 on the number line. Which tens value is it closer to, 80 or 90?

   90

B Round each number to the nearest ten.

1. 18 **20**   2. 86 **90**
3. 33 **30**   4. 5 **10**
5. 57 **60**   6. 60 **60**
7. 74 **70**   8. 49 **50**
9. 22 **20**   10. 91 **90**

116

C Round each car's number to the nearest ten.

Car	Car Number	Nearest Ten
	94	90
	11	10
	19	20
	58	60

D Round these numbers to the nearest ten.

1. 25 **30**   2. 188 **190**
3. 177 **180**   4. 834 **830**
5. 350 **350**   6. 856 **860**
7. 215 **220**   8. 567 **570**
9. 463 **460**   10. 999 **1000**

117

Evenly Split

Mike really likes pizza! His favorite pizza has mushrooms, pepperoni, and eyeballs on it. He eats a slice of pizza with mushrooms and eyeballs.

A Mike took his slice from the pizza below. Answer questions about the pizza by writing fractions out in words.

1. What fraction of the pizza did Mike take? **one sixth**

2. What fraction of the pizza is left over? **five sixths**

3. What fraction of the pizza has pepperoni? **four sixths or two thirds**

4. What fraction of the pizza has mushrooms? **four sixths or two thirds**

5. What fraction of the pizza has eyeballs? **one sixth**

6. What fraction of the pizza has pepperoni and mushrooms? **two sixths or one third**

118

B Mike ordered pizzas for the Oozma Kappa team.

1. Draw mushrooms on two thirds of this pizza.

2. If Mike eats one slice of this pizza, what fraction is left? Write out the fraction using words.

   two thirds

3. Draw pepperoni slices on four quarters of this pizza.

4. If Mike wants the biggest slice of pizza, should he choose a slice of mushroom pizza or pepperoni pizza? How do you know?

   Mushroom pizza; the slice is one third, which is greater than one quarter.

119

Fearless Fractions

Skulls are an important symbol of *Día de los Muertos*, or Day of the Dead. The skulls represent the people who are being remembered. There are many skulls on the Rivera family's altar.

A Use words to write fractions for the set of skulls.

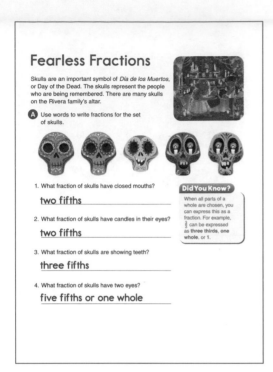

1. What fraction of skulls have closed mouths?

two fifths

2. What fraction of skulls have candles in their eyes?

two fifths

3. What fraction of skulls are showing teeth?

three fifths

4. What fraction of skulls have two eyes?

five fifths or one whole

Did You Know?

When all parts of a whole are chosen, you can express this as a fraction. For example, $\frac{3}{3}$ can be expressed as **three thirds**, **one whole**, or 1.

120

B Examine these Rivera family members who can be found in the Land of the Dead.

1. What fraction of family members shown wear earrings?

two fourths or one half

2. What fraction of family members shown are women?

three fourths

3. What fraction of family members shown are men?

one fourth

4. What fraction of family members shown can be found in the Land of the Dead?

four fourths or one whole

121

Let's Share

Bonnie got a lollipop from the carnival. She wants $\frac{2}{8}$ of the lollipop. She wants to share $\frac{1}{4}$ of the lollipop.

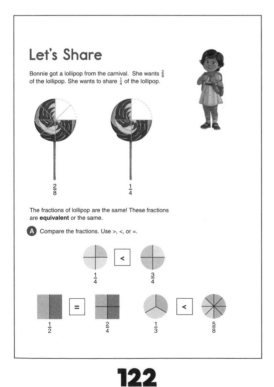

$\frac{2}{8}$ $\frac{1}{4}$

The fractions of lollipop are the same! These fractions are **equivalent** or the same.

A Compare the fractions. Use >, <, or =.

$\frac{1}{4}$ < $\frac{3}{4}$

$\frac{1}{2}$ = $\frac{2}{4}$ $\frac{1}{3}$ < $\frac{5}{8}$

122

B Write the fraction for each figure. Then, compare using <, >, or =.

$\frac{1}{2}$ = $\frac{2}{4}$ $\frac{2}{3}$ < $\frac{3}{4}$

$\frac{1}{5}$ < $\frac{2}{5}$ $\frac{3}{4}$ < $\frac{7}{8}$

$\frac{2}{3}$ > $\frac{1}{4}$ $\frac{5}{8}$ < $\frac{8}{10}$

123

234

© Disney/Pixar

Take Note

Miguel loves music. He enjoys singing and playing the guitar. Music has notes that are described as fractions, such as $\frac{1}{2}$ notes or $\frac{1}{4}$ notes. Which note do you think is held for longer? Think about which one is bigger.

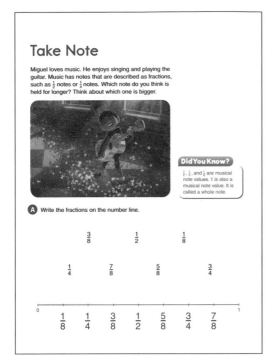

Did You Know?

$\frac{1}{2}$, $\frac{1}{4}$, and $\frac{1}{8}$ are musical note values. 1 is also a musical note value. It is called a whole note.

A Write the fractions on the number line.

$\frac{3}{8}$ $\frac{1}{2}$ $\frac{1}{8}$

$\frac{1}{4}$ $\frac{7}{8}$ $\frac{5}{8}$ $\frac{3}{4}$

0 — $\frac{1}{8}$ — $\frac{1}{4}$ — $\frac{3}{8}$ — $\frac{1}{2}$ — $\frac{5}{8}$ — $\frac{3}{4}$ — $\frac{7}{8}$ — 1

124

B Represent both fractions by shading the fraction strip. Circle the greater fraction.

1. $\boxed{\frac{4}{5}}$

$\frac{2}{3}$

2. $\frac{2}{4}$

$\boxed{\frac{3}{5}}$

3. $\boxed{\frac{1}{3}}$

$\frac{1}{4}$

4. $\frac{3}{5}$

$\boxed{\frac{3}{4}}$

5. How did you determine which fraction is greater?

I knew the fraction was greater when more of the fraction strip was shaded.

125

Money, Money, Money

Hamm is collecting money for Bonnie to spend at the carnival.

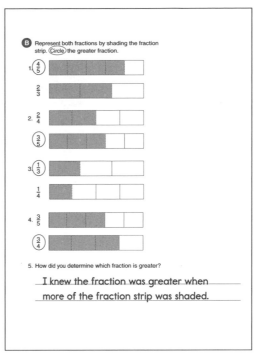

A Use words to write each amount. The first one is done for you.

1. $1.75 one dollar and seventy-five cents

2. $2.50 two dollars and fifty cents

3. $2.80 two dollars and eighty cents

4. $3.15 three dollars and fifteen cents

5. $5.35 five dollars and thirty-five cents

6. $7.90 seven dollars and ninety cents

Did You Know?

In the United States, money amounts are written using a dollar sign ($). The dollar sign is placed to the left of the amount ($7.62). If an amount is less than a dollar, you can still use the dollar sign. For example, **thirty-five cents** can be written as 35¢ or $0.35.

126

B Write the value for each group of coins and bills.

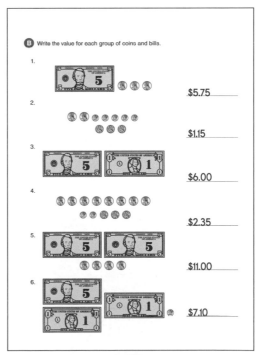

1. $5.75

2. $1.15

3. $6.00

4. $2.35

5. $11.00

6. $7.10

127

Counting Ahead

Mike is ready to start studying! He borrows 10 books from the library each day.

A Use the chart to answer the following questions.

Write in the missing numbers on the chart.

10	20	30	40	50	60	70	80	90	100
110	120	130	140	150	160	170	180	190	200
210	220	230	240	250	260	270	280	290	300
310	320	330	340	350	360	370	380	390	400
410	420	430	440	450	460	470	480	490	500
510	520	530	540	550	560	570	580	590	600
610	620	630	640	650	660	670	680	690	700
710	720	730	740	750	760	770	780	790	800
810	820	830	840	850	860	870	880	890	900
910	920	930	940	950	960	970	980	990	1000

B Use the completed chart to help you skip count.

1. Start at 210 and count forward by 10s to 300.

210, 220, 230, 240, 250, 260, 270, 280, 290, 300

2. Start at 850 and count forward by 10s to 1000.

850, 860, 870, 880, 890, 900, 910, 920, 930, 940, 950, 960, 970, 980, 990, 1000

128

C Mike has a big test coming up. He borrows 25 books each day. Use the number lines to practice counting forward by 25s.

1. If Mike borrows 25 books every day for eight days, how many books does he have? **200**

2. Start at 300 and count forward by 25s to 575. Write the numbers you counted.

300, 325, 350, 375, 400, 425, 450, 475, 500, 525, 550, 575

3. Start at 675 and count forward by 25s to 1000. Write the numbers you counted.

675, 700, 725, 750, 775, 800, 825, 850, 875, 900, 925, 950, 975, 1000

4. Extend this pattern after 1000 for two more numbers. What are those numbers? **1025, 1050**

129

Skip to It!

It's time to clean up the track after Lightning McQueen's race. There are 100 tires to put away. The tires are in stacks of 10.

A Use a number line to count how many stacks need to be put away. Start at 100 and skip count backward by 10s.

Number of tire stacks that need to be put away: **10**

B Use the number line to skip count backward.

1. Count backward by 10s starting at 95 and ending at 65.

95, 85, 75, 65

> **Did You Know?**
> Skip counting is not just a helpful way to count numbers faster. It also helps you to see patterns.

2. Count backward by 10s starting at 77 and ending at 57.

77, 67, 57

3. Count backward by 10s starting at 82 and ending at 52.

82, 72, 62, 52

4. Count backward by 10s starting at 99 and ending at 59.

99, 89, 79, 69, 59

130

C Tickets to Lightning's next race, the Florida 500, are selling quickly. Use the number line to skip count backward by 5s.

1. Count backward by 5s starting from 100 and ending at 50.

100, 95, 90, 85, 80, 75, 70, 65, 60, 55, 50

2. Count backward by 5s starting at 75 and ending at 45.

75, 70, 65, 60, 55, 50, 45

3. Count backward by 5s starting at 54 and ending at 24.

54, 49, 44, 39, 34, 29, 24

4. Count backward by 5s starting at 43 and ending at 13.

43, 38, 33, 28, 23, 18, 13

D Complete the number patterns.

1. 368, 358, 348, 338, 328, 318, 308

2. 900, 800, 700, 600, 500, 400, 300

3. 586, 581, 576, 571, 566, 561, 556

131

Write On!

Every race car needs a number, even the ones at the Crazy Eight demolition derby. One of the derby stars is Miss Fritter. She uses the number 58. This number can be written out in words as **fifty-eight**.

A Review number words by writing the race car numbers using words.

1. 71 seventy-one

2. 88 eighty-eight

3. 97 ninety-seven

4. 29 twenty-nine

5. 13 thirteen

6. 12 twelve

7. 33 thirty-three

8. 0 zero

Did You Know?

As in all spelling, there are some exceptions to the way numbers are written. For example, the number 4 is spelled **four**, but the number 40 is spelled **forty**, without the u.

132

B Many fans watch the Crazy Eight demolition derby. Write out the number of fans in words.

1. 561 five hundred sixty-one

2. 244 two hundred forty-four

3. 746 seven hundred forty-six

4. 913 nine hundred thirteen

5. 188 one hundred eighty-eight

6. 399 three hundred ninety-nine

7. 608 six hundred eight

Hint

To write three-digit numbers in words, start with the hundreds, then the tens, and finally the ones.

C Complete the number patterns below.

1. six hundred, _five hundred_, _four hundred_, three hundred, two hundred

2. two, twelve, _twenty-two_, _thirty-two_, _forty-two_, fifty-two

3. three hundred forty-seven, _three hundred thirty-seven_, _three hundred twenty-seven_, _three hundred seventeen_, three hundred seven

133

Sheepish Sums

Bo Peep has lost her sheep. The Aliens want to help Bo Peep. They add cotton balls to their bodies to pretend to be sheep.

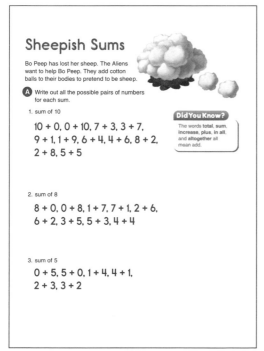

A Write out all the possible pairs of numbers for each sum.

1. sum of 10

10 + 0, 0 + 10, 7 + 3, 3 + 7, 9 + 1, 1 + 9, 6 + 4, 4 + 6, 8 + 2, 2 + 8, 5 + 5

Did You Know?

The words **total**, **sum**, **increase**, **plus**, **in all**, and **altogether** all mean add.

2. sum of 8

8 + 0, 0 + 8, 1 + 7, 7 + 1, 2 + 6, 6 + 2, 3 + 5, 5 + 3, 4 + 4

3. sum of 5

0 + 5, 5 + 0, 1 + 4, 4 + 1, 2 + 3, 3 + 2

134

B Calculate these sums using mental math.

1. 9 + 9 = __18__   2. 12 + 6 = __18__

3. 50 + 20 = __70__   4. 25 + 25 = __50__

5. 41 + 41 = __82__   6. 13 + 87 = __100__

7. 65 + 18 = __83__   8. 16 + 61 = __77__

9. 22 + 13 = __35__   10. 59 + 15 = __74__

Hint

Use the first number to make a number pair that adds to 10 with the second number. Then, complete the sum. For example, 5 + 6 = ? 6 can be expressed as 5 + 1.
5 + 5 = 10
10 + 1 = 11
5 + 6 = 11

C The Aliens find more cotton balls in the bathroom. They already have 18 cotton balls. If they add 6 more cotton balls, how many cotton balls do they have in total?

Use mental math to calculate the sum. Explain your answer.

Answers will vary. For example, recognize that 18 is 10 + 8. 8 + 6 is 14. Add 14 to 10 to get the answer of 24 cotton balls.

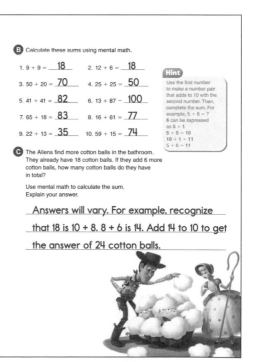

135

What's Left?

Bonnie wants to win some prizes at the carnival! She has 21 tickets and wants to turn some in for prizes.

A Use mental math strategies to help Bonnie. Explain how you got each answer.

1. How many tickets will be left if she spends 12 on a teddy bear?

$21 - 12 = \underline{9}$

Answers will vary. For example, use the friendly number strategy to recognize 12 is 10 + 2. First, 21 − 10 = 11. Then, 11 − 2 = 9.

2. How many tickets will be left if she spends 17 on a toy frog?

$21 - 17 = \underline{4}$

Answers will vary. For example, use the friendly number strategy to recognize 17 is 10 + 7. First, 21 − 10 = 11. Then, 11 − 7 = 4.

Hint

The **friendly number strategy** is a mental math strategy.
Example:
34 − 23 = ?
23 is 10 + 10 + 3
Subtract 10 from 34
34 − 10 = 24
Subtract 10 from 24
24 − 10 = 14
Subtract 3 from 14
14 − 3 = 11
So, 34 − 23 = 11

B Subtract using a mental math strategy.

1. $42 - 22 = \underline{20}$ 2. $19 - 12 = \underline{7}$

3. $34 - 14 = \underline{20}$ 4. $66 - 33 = \underline{30}$

5. $28 - 17 = \underline{11}$ 6. $44 - 23 = \underline{21}$

7. $38 - 21 = \underline{17}$ 8. $79 - 56 = \underline{23}$

9. $53 - 25 = \underline{28}$ 10. $50 - 25 = \underline{25}$

Hint

The **adding up strategy** is a mental math strategy.
Example:
34 − 23 = ?
You want to add up from 23 until you reach 34.
Add 7 to 23 to reach 30
23 + 7 = 30
Add 4 to 30 to reach 34
30 + 4 = 34
7 + 4 = 11
So, 34 − 23 = 11

C Now, Bonnie has 56 tickets she wants to spend. If she spends 14, how many does she have left? Use a mental math strategy to solve the problem. Explain how you got your answer.

Bonnie will have 42 tickets left. Answers will vary. For example, use a mental math strategy, like the friendly number strategy. First, recognize that 14 is 10+4. Then, subtract 10 from 56 to get 46. Then subtract 4 from 42 to get 42.

What's the Total?

Miguel's town is preparing for *Día de los Muertos* by hanging paper banners called *papel picado* from houses. Each street is decorated with many banners.

A Use regrouping to calculate the number of papel picado hanging along different streets. Show your work by drawing base ten blocks for each question.

1. $347 + 125 = \underline{472}$

Hundreds	Tens	Ones
▢▢ ▢▢	❘❘❘❘❘❘❘	▫ ▫

2. $132 + 228 = \underline{360}$

Hundreds	Tens	Ones
▢▢ ▢	❘❘❘❘❘❘	

B Calculate each sum.

1. $\begin{array}{r} 316 \\ + 422 \\ \hline 738 \end{array}$ 2. $\begin{array}{r} 334 \\ + 353 \\ \hline 687 \end{array}$ 3. $\begin{array}{r} 553 \\ + 116 \\ \hline 669 \end{array}$

4. $\begin{array}{r} 161 \\ + 125 \\ \hline 286 \end{array}$ 5. $\begin{array}{r} 722 \\ + 250 \\ \hline 972 \end{array}$ 6. $\begin{array}{r} 274 \\ + 210 \\ \hline 484 \end{array}$

7. $\begin{array}{r} 255 \\ + 236 \\ \hline 491 \end{array}$ 8. $\begin{array}{r} 326 \\ + 227 \\ \hline 553 \end{array}$ 9. $\begin{array}{r} 445 \\ + 149 \\ \hline 594 \end{array}$

C Miguel's town only has space to hang 800 papel picado. The townspeople hang 485 papel picado one night. They still have 287 more papel picado to hang. Is there enough space for these papel picado? Calculate and explain your answer.

485 papel picado + 287 papel picado equals 772 papel picado. There is enough room for these banners.

Hint

When you are adding numbers, you may need to regroup them. For example, 37 is 2 tens and 17 ones or 3 tens and 7 ones.

Driving Differences

Lightning McQueen wants to train on Fireball Beach. Cruz Ramirez follows him there, but she keeps getting stuck in the sand.

A Lightning reaches a top speed of 197 mi/h at Fireball Beach, while Cruz reaches 189 mi/h. What is the difference between their top speeds on the beach?

Did You Know?
Words like **difference**, **decrease**, **fewer**, and **how many more** all tell you to subtract.

$$\begin{array}{r} 197 \\ -\ 189 \\ \hline \end{array}$$
8 mi/h

B Calculate each difference.

1. $\begin{array}{r} 734 \\ -\ 432 \\ \hline \mathbf{302} \end{array}$
2. $\begin{array}{r} 889 \\ -\ 679 \\ \hline \mathbf{210} \end{array}$
3. $\begin{array}{r} 509 \\ -\ 105 \\ \hline \mathbf{404} \end{array}$

4. $\begin{array}{r} 462 \\ -\ 341 \\ \hline \mathbf{121} \end{array}$
5. $\begin{array}{r} 178 \\ -\ 126 \\ \hline \mathbf{52} \end{array}$
6. $\begin{array}{r} 377 \\ -\ 270 \\ \hline \mathbf{107} \end{array}$

140

---

7. $\begin{array}{r} 651 \\ -\ 417 \\ \hline \mathbf{234} \end{array}$
8. $\begin{array}{r} 563 \\ -\ 259 \\ \hline \mathbf{304} \end{array}$
9. $\begin{array}{r} 182 \\ -\ 175 \\ \hline \mathbf{7} \end{array}$

10. $\begin{array}{r} 271 \\ -\ 253 \\ \hline \mathbf{18} \end{array}$
11. $\begin{array}{r} 534 \\ -\ 426 \\ \hline \mathbf{108} \end{array}$
12. $\begin{array}{r} 494 \\ -\ 177 \\ \hline \mathbf{317} \end{array}$

13. $\begin{array}{r} 776 \\ -\ 558 \\ \hline \mathbf{218} \end{array}$
14. $\begin{array}{r} 338 \\ -\ 129 \\ \hline \mathbf{209} \end{array}$
15. $\begin{array}{r} 980 \\ -\ 351 \\ \hline \mathbf{629} \end{array}$

C Solve each word problem.

1. Cruz completes 290 practice laps in one week. Lightning completes 350 practice laps in one week. How many more practice laps does Lightning complete than Cruz?

Lightning McQueen completes 60 more practice laps.

2. The following week, Lightning completes 70 fewer practice laps and Cruz completes 50 more than each did the week before. How many more laps does Cruz complete than Lightning?

In the second week, Cruz completes 60 more practice laps.

141

Working Together

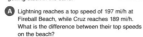

The Green Army Men line up in three pairs to carry a baby monitor downstairs. Three pairs can be expressed as $2 + 2 + 2$ or 3×2.

A Use the number lines to help you skip count, add, and multiply.

1. Show $2 + 2 + 2$ on the number line.

Write the addition sentence.
$2 + 2 + 2 = 6$

Did You Know?
A **multiplication fact**, or multiplication sentence, has two types of numbers: **factors** and the **product**. In the equation $7 \times 5 = 35$, 7 and 5 are the factors. 35 is the product.

Write the multiplication fact.
$3 \times 2 = 6$

2. Show $3 + 3 + 3$ on the number line.

Write the addition sentence.
$3 + 3 + 3 = 9$

Write the multiplication fact.
$3 \times 3 = 9$

142

B Fill in the blanks with the correct factors. Calculate each product. You can use the number line to help you.

1. **6** $\times 2 = 12$
2. $2 \times 8 =$ **16**
3. $3 \times 7 =$ **21**
4. $4 \times 6 =$ **24**
5. $4 \times 5 =$ **20**
6. $6 \times$ **7** $= 42$
7. $5 \times 6 =$ **30**
8. $5 \times 3 =$ **15**
9. $7 \times$ **4** $= 28$
10. $7 \times 7 =$ **49**

Hint
Start at 0 when using a number line to show repeated addition.

C Draw a picture to represent each set of words. Write a multiplication fact for each set.

1. 6 groups of 3 Aliens

$3 \times 6 = 18$

2. 4 groups of 4 Aliens

$4 \times 4 = 16$

143

© Disney/Pixar

239

Set It Up!

It is time to set up traffic cones at the Florida International Super Speedway.

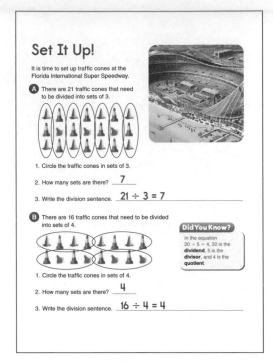

A There are 21 traffic cones that need to be divided into sets of 3.

1. Circle the traffic cones in sets of 3.

2. How many sets are there? __7__

3. Write the division sentence. __21 ÷ 3 = 7__

B There are 16 traffic cones that need to be divided into sets of 4.

Did You Know?

In the equation 20 ÷ 5 = 4, 20 is the **dividend**, 5 is the **divisor**, and 4 is the **quotient**.

1. Circle the traffic cones in sets of 4.

2. How many sets are there? __4__

3. Write the division sentence. __16 ÷ 4 = 4__

144

C Draw a model to help you solve each problem. Circle the sets. Then, write the division sentence.

1. 20 traffic cones divided into 5 sets

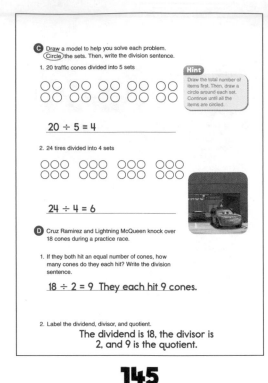

Hint

Draw the total number of items first. Then, draw a circle around each set. Continue until all the items are circled.

__20 ÷ 5 = 4__

2. 24 tires divided into 4 sets

__24 ÷ 4 = 6__

D Cruz Ramirez and Lightning McQueen knock over 18 cones during a practice race.

1. If they both hit an equal number of cones, how many cones do they each hit? Write the division sentence.

__18 ÷ 2 = 9__ They each hit 9 cones.

2. Label the dividend, divisor, and quotient.

The dividend is 18, the divisor is 2, and 9 is the quotient.

145

More and More

Mike and Sulley take scaring very seriously. They want to be the best scaring team at Monsters University!

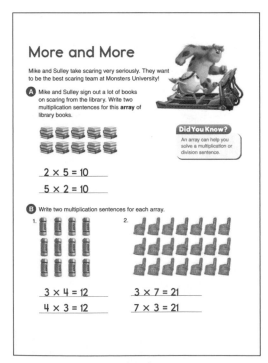

A Mike and Sulley sign out a lot of books on scaring from the library. Write two multiplication sentences for this **array** of library books.

Did You Know?

An array can help you solve a multiplication or division sentence.

__2 × 5 = 10__

__5 × 2 = 10__

B Write two multiplication sentences for each array.

1.

__3 × 4 = 12__

__4 × 3 = 12__

2.

__3 × 7 = 21__

__7 × 3 = 21__

146

C Solve each multiplication fact. Sketch an array for each multiplication fact.

1. 2 × 6 = __12__

2. 3 × 3 = __9__

3. 4 × 4 = __12__

D How many multiplication sentences can you create for the product 36? Write all of the possible multiplication sentences below.

Hint

You could use blocks or beads to model arrays of 36.

9 sentences: 1 × 36, 36 × 1, 2 × 18, 18 × 2, 3 × 12, 12 × 3, 4 × 9, 9 × 4, 6 × 6

147

Fast Facts

A You have to be fast to be a racer! Solve these multiplication facts as fast as Lightning McQueen races.

$2 \times 2 =$ __4__ $3 \times 4 =$ __12__ $5 \times 6 =$ __30__

$8 \times 2 =$ __16__ $7 \times 6 =$ __42__ $4 \times 4 =$ __16__

$5 \times 3 =$ __15__ $3 \times 7 =$ __21__ $2 \times 9 =$ __18__

148

$2 \times 3 =$ __6__ $0 \times 6 =$ __0__ $8 \times 10 =$ __80__

$8 \times 4 =$ __32__ $4 \times 6 =$ __24__ $3 \times 8 =$ __24__

$5 \times 9 =$ __45__ $10 \times 2 =$ __20__ $5 \times 2 =$ __10__

$3 \times 6 =$ __18__ $4 \times 7 =$ __28__ $5 \times 4 =$ __20__

$9 \times 10 =$ __90__ $3 \times 3 =$ __9__ $8 \times 7 =$ __56__

$0 \times 10 =$ __0__ $9 \times 2 =$ __18__ $5 \times 7 =$ __35__

$4 \times 2 =$ __8__ $5 \times 5 =$ __25__ $8 \times 9 =$ __72__

149

Going Backward

Miguel wants to go back to the Land of the Living. Going backward along a number line can help you divide.

A Use the number line to model division. Write a division sentence.

0 1 2 3 4 5 6 7 8 9 10 11 12

1. Start at 8 and jump backward by 2s to 0.

$8 \div 2 = 4$

2. Start at 10 and jump backward by 2s to 0.

$10 \div 2 = 5$

3. Start at 9 and jump backward by 3s to 0.

$9 \div 3 = 3$

4. Start at 8 and jump backward by 4s to 0.

$8 \div 4 = 2$

5. Start at 6 and jump backward by 3s to 0.

$6 \div 3 = 2$

Did You Know?
When you use a number line for division, the starting number is the dividend. The size of your backward jumps is your divisor. The number of jumps along the number line is your quotient.

B Choose one of the questions above. Label the dividend, divisor, and quotient.

Answers will vary. For example, 8 is the dividend, 2 is the divisor, and 4 is the quotient.

150

C Use the number line to solve the division sentences.

0   10   20   30

1. $21 \div 7 =$ __3__   2. $15 \div 5 =$ __3__
3. $16 \div 4 =$ __4__   4. $18 \div 9 =$ __2__
5. $25 \div 5 =$ __5__   6. $14 \div 2 =$ __7__
7. $24 \div 6 =$ __4__   8. $20 \div 4 =$ __5__
9. $30 \div 3 =$ __10__   10. $21 \div 3 =$ __7__

D Ernesto de la Cruz shows Miguel the guitars his fans sent him. There are 24 guitars placed in 3 rows.

1. How many guitars are in each row?   __8__

2. If the 24 guitars are rearranged in 4 rows, how many guitars would be in each row?   __6__

3. Write the division sentence for this new arrangement.

   $24 \div 4 = 6$

4. Ernesto receives 4 more guitars. How many sets of 4 can now be made? Explain your answer.

   $28 \div 4 = 7$

   28 can be divided by 4 seven times.

151

Buy and Sell!

Andy's mom is having a yard sale and thinks about selling some of Andy's toys.

A Calculate how much a customer might pay for each combination.

$2.05

$3.75

1. Hamm and Rex __$5.80__

2. the Green Army Men and the Aliens __$6.49__

$4.99

3. Hamm and the Green Army Men __$7.04__

$1.50

4. Rex and the Aliens __$5.25__

Did You Know?
Any numbers to the right of the decimal are less than a whole dollar. Numbers to the left of the decimal are whole dollars.

B Compare the costs of different toys. Show your work. Explain your answer.

1. How much more does Rex cost than Hamm?

_____ $1.70 _____

152

---

2. How much more do the Green Army Men cost than the Aliens?

_____ $3.49 _____

3. How much more does Rex cost than the Aliens?

_____ $2.25 _____

4. How much more do the Green Army Men cost than Hamm?

_____ $2.94 _____

C A neighbor wants to buy some toys. He has $7.00. Would he have enough money to buy Hamm, the Aliens, and Rex? Show your work. Explain your answer.

If Hamm costs $2.05, the Aliens cost $1.50, and Rex costs $3.75, the total for all three is $7.30. Sid does not have enough money.

Luckily, Andy's mom does not sell any of Andy's beloved toys!

153

Again and Again

Patterns are everywhere in the Land of the Living. They are everywhere in the Land of the Dead, too!

A Identify the **attributes** of each pattern using these words: size, color, orientation, shape, number.

1.

__shape, color, number__

2.

__size__

Did You Know?
Attributes are features that you can describe, such as shape, size, number, color, and orientation. When you are describing patterns in words, identify the pattern's attributes and how they change.

3.

__color, number__

Hint
Orientation refers to which way an object is facing.

4.

__orientation__

154

B Identify the attributes of each pattern. Then, extend each pattern.

1.

__size, orientation__

2.

__shape, color__

C Create your own pattern using three attributes. Describe the attributes of your pattern.

__Answers will vary. The pattern must have__ __three attributes and be described correctly.__

155

Friends Rule!

Lightning McQueen enjoys hanging out with the Radiator Springs gang.

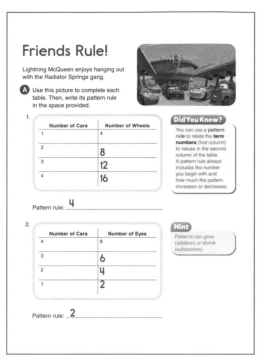

A Use this picture to complete each table. Then, write its pattern rule in the space provided.

1.

Number of Cars	Number of Wheels
1	4
2	8
3	12
4	16

Pattern rule: 4

Did You Know?
You can use a **pattern rule** to relate the **term numbers** (first column) to values in the second column of the table. A pattern rule always includes the number you begin with and how much the pattern increases or decreases.

2.

Number of Cars	Number of Eyes
4	8
3	6
2	4
1	2

Hint
Patterns can grow (addition) or shrink (subtraction).

Pattern rule: 2

156

B Follow the pattern rule to complete each table.

1. Start at 3 and increase by 4.

Term Number	Number in Pattern
1	3
2	7
3	11
4	15

Hint
Use skip counting to complete the patterns.

2. Start at 25 and decrease by 5.

Term Number	Number in Pattern
1	25
2	20
3	15
4	10

C Create your own pattern and pattern rule.

Pattern rule: **Answers will vary. Term number and pattern rule must be consistent.**

Term Number	Number in Pattern
1	
2	
3	
4	

157

Studying Graphs

Mike and Sulley love being students at Monsters University!

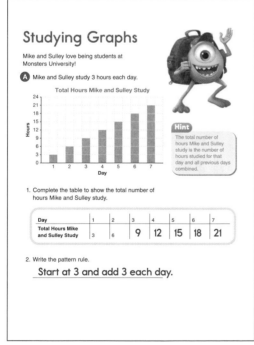

A Mike and Sulley study 3 hours each day.

Total Hours Mike and Sulley Study

(bar graph with Hours axis 0–24, Day axis 1–7)

Hint
The total number of hours Mike and Sulley study is the number of hours studied for that day and all previous days combined.

1. Complete the table to show the total number of hours Mike and Sulley study.

Day	1	2	3	4	5	6	7
Total Hours Mike and Sulley Study	3	6	9	12	15	18	21

2. Write the pattern rule.

Start at 3 and add 3 each day.

158

B Mike and Sulley study for 5 more days. Extend the number pattern by 5 more days.

Day	8	9	10	11	12
Total Hours Mike and Sulley Study	24	27	30	33	36

C Complete a bar graph to represent the total number of hours Mike and Sulley study from day 8 to day 12.

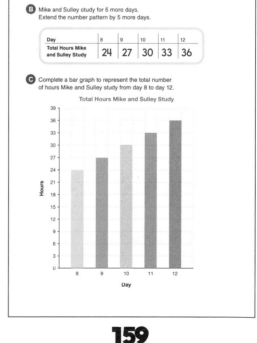

Total Hours Mike and Sulley Study

(bar graph with Hours axis 0–39, Day axis 8–12)

159

What's Missing?

Woody and Forky are missing! Buzz is looking for them. In addition and subtraction, numbers sometimes go missing, too!

A Find the missing number for each subtraction sentence.

1	2	3	4	5	6	7	8	9	10
11	12	13	14	15	16	17	18	19	20
21	22	23	24	25	26	27	28	29	30
31	32	33	34	35	36	37	38	39	40
41	42	43	44	45	46	47	48	49	50
51	52	53	54	55	56	57	58	59	60
61	62	63	64	65	66	67	68	69	70
71	72	73	74	75	76	77	78	79	80
81	82	83	84	85	86	87	88	89	90
91	92	93	94	95	96	97	98	99	100

1. $23 - \underline{2} = 21$ 2. $29 - \underline{15} = 14$

3. $84 - \underline{22} = 62$ 4. $73 - \underline{14} = 59$

5. $57 - \underline{19} = 38$ 6. $63 - \underline{22} = 41$

7. $\underline{67} - 20 = 47$ 8. $\underline{44} - 9 = 35$

Hint
When the second number is missing, add up from the answer to the first number. If the first number is missing, add the second number and the answer. A 100-chart can help you with this.

160

B Find the missing number for each addition sentence.

0 2 4 6 8 10 12 14 16 18 20

1. $6 + \underline{3} = 9$ 2. $9 + \underline{5} = 14$

3. $\underline{11} + 5 = 16$ 4. $\underline{7} + 3 = 10$

5. $7 + \underline{11} = 18$ 6. $\underline{8} + 12 = 20$

7. $6 + \underline{5} = 11$ 8. $\underline{2} + 17 = 19$

9. $\underline{10} + 7 = 17$ 10. $\underline{4} + 8 = 12$

Hint
Use the number line to help you.

C Bonnie buys a roll of star stickers. The roll has 57 stickers. When she gets home, she counts only 33 stickers. How many stickers went missing? Write the number sentence and explain your answer.

$57 - 33 = 24$. Answers will vary. For example, using a mental math strategy, find the missing number. Break down 33 into 30 and 3. $57 - 30 = 27$. Then subtract 3 to get 24.

161

One or None

Many monsters at Monsters University do not have tails. Ms. Squibbles doesn't have one either!

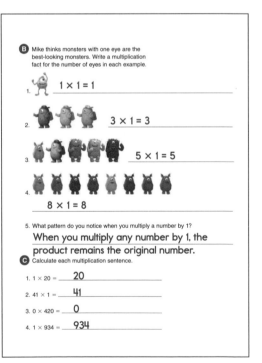

A Write a multiplication fact for the number of tails in each example. The first one is done for you.

1. $3 \times 0 = 0$

2. $4 \times 0 = 0$

3. $4 \times 0 = 0$

4. $7 \times 0 = 0$

5. What do you notice when you multiply a number by 0?

The product is always 0.

162

B Mike thinks monsters with one eye are the best-looking monsters. Write a multiplication fact for the number of eyes in each example.

1. $1 \times 1 = 1$

2. $3 \times 1 = 3$

3. $5 \times 1 = 5$

4. $8 \times 1 = 8$

5. What pattern do you notice when you multiply a number by 1?

When you multiply any number by 1, the product remains the original number.

C Calculate each multiplication sentence.

1. $1 \times 20 = \underline{20}$

2. $41 \times 1 = \underline{41}$

3. $0 \times 420 = \underline{0}$

4. $1 \times 934 = \underline{934}$

163

244

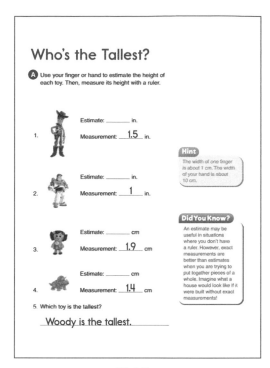

Who's the Tallest?

A Use your finger or hand to estimate the height of each toy. Then, measure its height with a ruler.

1. Estimate: _____ in.
   Measurement: __1.5__ in.

Hint
The width of one finger is about 1 cm. The width of your hand is about 10 cm.

2. Estimate: _____ in.
   Measurement: __1__ in.

3. Estimate: _____ cm
   Measurement: __1.9__ cm

Did You Know?
An estimate may be useful in situations where you don't have a ruler. However, exact measurements are better than estimates when you are trying to put together pieces of a whole. Imagine what a house would look like if it were built without exact measurements!

4. Estimate: _____ cm
   Measurement: __1.4__ cm

5. Which toy is the tallest?

   __Woody is the tallest.__

164

B Estimate and measure other items in inches.

1. width of this book   Estimate: _____   Measurement: __7.7 in.__

2. length of this book   Estimate: _____   Measurement: __10.6 in.__

3. height of the Hint box   Estimate: _____   Measurement: __1.2 in.__

C Find objects at home that you estimate have lengths of 20 cm, 40 cm, and 60 cm. Then, use a ruler to measure them.

1. 20 cm   Object: _____   Exact measurement: _____

2. 40 cm   Object: _____   Exact measurement: _____

3. 60 cm   Object: _____   Exact measurement: _____

Answers will vary.

4. Explain how you estimated the length of each object.

   _____

   Answers will vary.

5. Which of your estimates came closest to the actual measurement?

   _____

   Answers will vary.

165

Made to Measure

Mike packs everything he needs for school, including a ruler!

A Draw the objects listed below. Use Mike's ruler to help you.

1. A pencil that is $3\frac{1}{4}$ in. long.

   Drawings will vary. Should match measurements given.

2. A monster that is $5\frac{1}{2}$ in. long.

3. An eraser that is 2 in. long.

4. A straw that is $4\frac{3}{4}$ in. long.

166

B Use a ruler to measure the height of each monster's class photo. Number these photos in order from shortest to tallest. The first one is done for you.

__1__ in. (1)   Mike

__1.9__ in. (3)   Art

__1.2__ in. (2)   Nan

__3.5__ in. (6)   Dean Hardscrabble

__2.3__ in. (4)   Don

__3__ in. (5)   Sulley

167

How Heavy Is a Scare Pig?

Archie the Scare Pig steals Mike's Monsters University hat! Mike tries to stop him from getting away, but Archie is stronger and heavier than Mike thought.

Archie's **mass** can be measured in pounds or kilograms. Mike's hat can be measured in ounces or grams.

A Choose a unit of measurement for each item. (Circle) your choice.

1. suitcase   grams   (kilograms)

2. Scare Games flyer   (ounces)   pounds

3. backpack   grams   (kilograms)

4. movie ticket   (ounces)   pounds

5. map   (grams)   kilograms

6. textbook   ounces   (pounds)

B Think about the mass for each animal.

elephant   blue whale   robin   lion

human adult male   bee   wolf

168

---

1. List the animals from heaviest to lightest.

blue whale, elephant, lion, human
adult male, wolf, robin, bee

2. How could you find out if you are correct?

Research all the weights from a
book or the Internet.

C Ms. Squibbles has two bottles of laundry detergent. One bottle is 1,075 g. The other is 1 kg. Which bottle weighs more? Explain your answer.

The bottle with 1,075
g weighs more. This is
because 1 kg is the same
as 1,000 g.

169

Fill 'er Up

At Flo's V8 Cafe, gasoline for the cars is stored in gas pumps. The **capacity** of liquids can be measured in quarts and gallons or milliliters and liters.

A Choose a unit of measurement for each item. (Circle) your choice.

1. gasoline

   quarts   (gallons)

2. oil barrels

   milliliters   (liters)

3. small oil can

   (quarts)   gallons

4. Lightning McQueen's gas tank

   milliliters   (liters)

5. Piston Cup trophy

   quarts   (gallons)

6. small paint can

   (milliliters)   liters

170

B Convert these measurements from mL to L or L to mL.

1. __2,000__ mL = 2 L

2. 3,000 mL = __3__ L

3. 9,000 mL = __9__ L

4. __6,000__ mL = 6 L

5. __10,000__ mL = 10 L

C Order the capacities from least to greatest using numbers 1 to 4.

1. 2,690 mL laundry detergent jug

2. 500 mL juice bottle

3. 1 L measuring cup

4. 2 L milk jug

   __2__   __3__   __4__   __1__

171

Ready to Race!

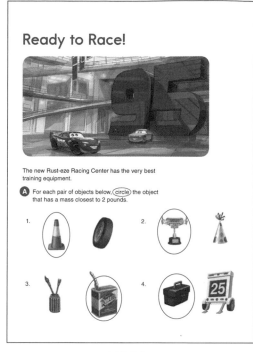

The new Rust-eze Racing Center has the very best training equipment.

A For each pair of objects below, (circle) the object that has a mass closest to 2 pounds.

1.
2.
3.
4.

172

B These are some objects you might find in your own home. (Circle) the object that has a capacity closest to 1 liter.

1.
2.
MILK
3.
4.
5.

C List two objects for each question.

1. Which objects in your home have a mass of about 2 pounds?

   Answers will vary. Think of a reasonable object, like a plant.

2. Which objects in your home have a capacity of about 1 liter?

   Answers will vary. Think of a reasonable object, like a water bottle.

173

Measure Up!

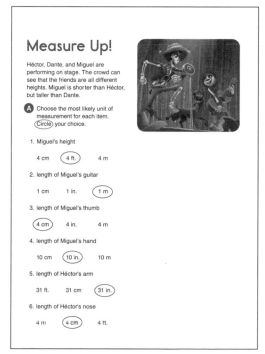

Héctor, Dante, and Miguel are performing on stage. The crowd can see that the friends are all different heights. Miguel is shorter than Héctor, but taller than Dante.

A Choose the most likely unit of measurement for each item. (Circle) your choice.

1. Miguel's height

   4 cm   (4 ft.)   4 m

2. length of Miguel's guitar

   1 cm   1 in.   (1 m)

3. length of Miguel's thumb

   (4 cm)   4 in.   4 m

4. length of Miguel's hand

   10 cm   (10 in.)   10 m

5. length of Héctor's arm

   31 ft.   31 cm   (31 in.)

6. length of Héctor's nose

   4 m   (4 cm)   4 ft.

174

B Draw a (circle) around the most likely capacity for each item.

1. juice box	20 mL	(200 mL)	2 L
2. pop can	35 mL	(350 mL)	3 L
3. carton of milk	(1 L)	3 L	10 L
4. bottle of soda	10 mL	(2 L)	10 L
5. drinking cup	10 mL	(200 mL)	1 L
6. spoon	(5 mL)	50 mL	500 mL
7. swimming pool	5 L	50 L	(5000 L)
8. large cooking pot	2 mL	200 mL	(4 L)
9. tube of toothpaste	10 mL	(100 mL)	1 L
10. bottle of dish soap	1 mL	(1 L)	10 L

Hint
Use items you know to help you visualize capacity. For example, a bottle of water is 500 mL.

C Answer the following questions.

1. What happens when you pour 1 gallon of milk into a 2 quart measuring cup?

   The milk will spill out if you try to pour it all in. Half of the milk will be spilled.

2. If your garden needs 1 L of water each day and your watering can holds 250 mL, how many times do you have to fill up your watering can?

   1000 mL is equal to 1 L. I will need to fill up my watering can 4 times to water the garden.

175

© Disney/Pixar

247

Catch Me If You Can!

Lightning enjoys driving around the **perimeter** of a track. Sometimes, he moves so fast that it looks like he is covering the whole **area** of the track at once.

A Calculate the perimeter of each shape. Then calculate the area. Each square on the grid represents 1 in².

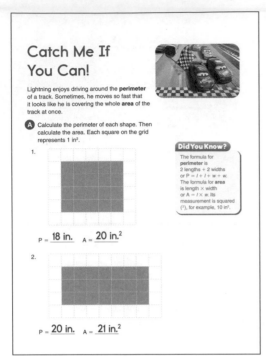

Did You Know?

The formula for **perimeter** is 2 lengths + 2 widths or $P = l + l + w + w$. The formula for **area** is length × width or $A = l \times w$. Its measurement is squared (²), for example, 10 in².

1. P = __18 in.__ A = __20 in.²__

2. P = __20 in.__ A = __21 in.²__

176

B The perimeter of a rectangle is 14 ft. and the area is 10 ft². Draw the rectangle. Label the width and the length.

length 5 ft.
width 2 ft.

C Lightning races around a track with an area of 24 m². Write all combinations of length and width that will equal an area of 24 m².

length 24 m, width 1 m
length 12 m, width 2 m
length 8 m, width 3 m
length 6 m, width 4 m
length 4 m, width 6 m
length 3 m, width 8 m
length 2 m, width 12 m
length 1 m, width 24 m

177

It's All about the Volume

Sulley has one textbook that is so big it might not fit in his backpack!

A Calculate the **volume** of each book.

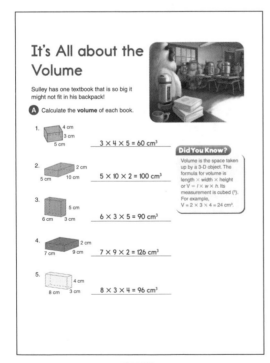

1. 4 cm, 3 cm, 5 cm $3 \times 4 \times 5 = 60 \text{ cm}^3$

Did You Know?

Volume is the space taken up by a 3-D object. The formula for volume is length × width × height or $V = l \times w \times h$. Its measurement is cubed (³). For example, $V = 2 \times 3 \times 4 = 24 \text{ cm}^3$.

2. 2 cm, 5 cm, 10 cm $5 \times 10 \times 2 = 100 \text{ cm}^3$

3. 5 cm, 6 cm, 3 cm $6 \times 3 \times 5 = 90 \text{ cm}^3$

4. 2 cm, 7 cm, 9 cm $7 \times 9 \times 2 = 126 \text{ cm}^3$

5. 4 cm, 8 cm, 3 cm $8 \times 3 \times 4 = 96 \text{ cm}^3$

178

B Complete the measurements table. Calculate Volume #1 using the first set of dimensions. Calculate Volume #2 using the change in dimension.

Hint

Use your pencil to mark the change in dimension to help you recalculate.

Changing Measurements

	Original Dimensions			Volume #1	Change	Volume #2
	Length	Width	Height			
1.	3 in.	4 in.	6 in.	72 in.³	height to 3 in.	36 in.³
2.	5 cm	2 cm	8 cm	80 cm³	length to 10 cm	160 cm³
3.	2 in.	4 in.	3 in.	24 in.³	width to 2 in.	12 in.³
4.	3 ft.	8 ft.	2 ft.	48 ft.³	length to 6 ft.	96 ft.³
5.	4 m	3 m	5 m	60 m³	height to 10 m	120 m³

C Write a sentence to answer each question.

1. What happens to the volume when a dimension is doubled?

   When a dimension doubles, the volume also doubles.

2. What happens to the volume when a dimension is halved?

   When a dimension halves, the volume also halves.

179

248

© Disney/Pixar

Good Timing

The toys are planning a schedule of activities while Bonnie is at school.

A Match the timed activity with the clock showing the correct time.

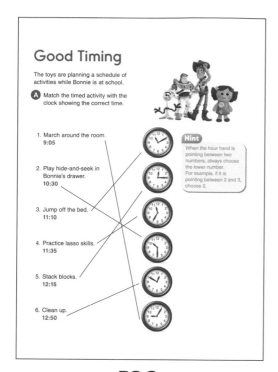

1. March around the room.
   9:05

2. Play hide-and-seek in Bonnie's drawer.
   10:30

3. Jump off the bed.
   11:10

4. Practice lasso skills.
   11:35

5. Stack blocks.
   12:15

6. Clean up.
   12:50

Hint
When the hour hand is pointing between two numbers, always choose the lower number. For example, if it is pointing between 2 and 3, choose 2.

180

B Show the correct time on each blank clock.

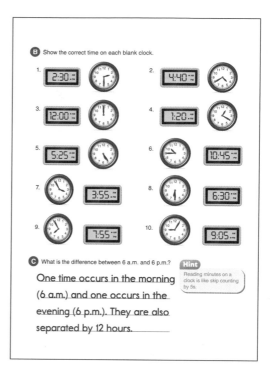

1. 2:30
2. 4:40
3. 12:00
4. 1:20
5. 5:25
6. 10:45
7. 3:55
8. 6:30
9. 7:55
10. 9:05

C What is the difference between 6 a.m. and 6 p.m.?

One time occurs in the morning (6 a.m.) and one occurs in the evening (6 p.m.). They are also separated by 12 hours.

Hint
Reading minutes on a clock is like skip counting by 5s.

181

Simply Symmetrical

Lightning McQueen enters the Crazy Eight demolition derby.

A Examine the Crazy Eight Track. Draw any **lines of symmetry**.

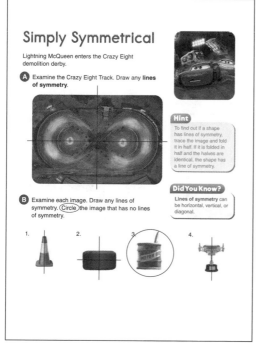

Hint
To find out if a shape has lines of symmetry, trace the image and fold it in half. If it is folded in half and the halves are identical, the shape has a line of symmetry.

B Examine each image. Draw any lines of symmetry. Circle the image that has no lines of symmetry.

Did You Know?
Lines of symmetry can be horizontal, vertical, or diagonal.

1.
2.
3.
4.

182

C Draw lines of symmetry on the shapes below. Describe the lines of symmetry. The first one is done for you.

1. There are two lines of symmetry. One is vertical and the other one is horizontal.

2. There are four lines of symmetry. One vertical, one horizontal, and two diagonal.

3. There are three lines of symmetry. One vertical and two diagonal.

4. There are no lines of symmetry.

D Draw a symmetrical object. Show the lines of symmetry. Describe the lines of symmetry.

Answers will vary. Make sure to draw all possible lines of symmetry (horizontal, vertical, and diagonal).

183

Shape Up!

The Green Army Men defend the block castle from a fire-breathing dragon, played by Rex. What shapes can you identify in the castle?

A Match each name to the correct shape.

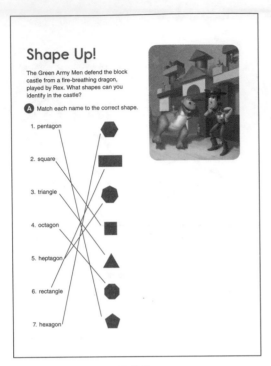

1. pentagon
2. square
3. triangle
4. octagon
5. heptagon
6. rectangle
7. hexagon

184

B Use the shapes to complete the Venn diagrams. Write the letters representing the shapes in the Venn diagrams.

Hint
A Venn diagram shows which features are shared and which are different. If the shape shares both characteristics, it goes in the overlap section of the Venn diagram.

1. Four Sides or More   Two Lines of Symmetry

    a e f g | b c

2. Four Right Angles   Equal Side Lengths

    c | b | a d e f g

3. Four Sides   Equal Side Lengths

    c | b | a e g | d f

185

Mirror Images

This guitar is shown in a **vertical reflection**.

Here, the guitar is shown in a **horizontal reflection**.

Did You Know?
You can draw a line of **reflection** to check if a shape has been reflected horizontally, vertically, or diagonally.

Hint
Use the dot paper to help you draw the missing half.

A Trace the dotted line to show the vertical line of reflection. Draw a vertical reflection of each picture.

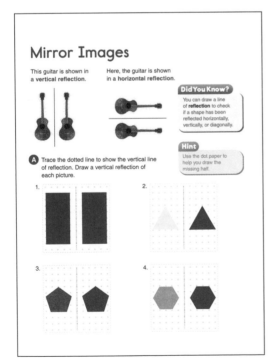

1.
2.
3.
4.

186

B Trace the dotted horizontal line of reflection. Draw a horizontal reflection of each picture.

1.
2.
3.
4.

C Trace the vertical line of reflection. Reflect this image vertically. Now, trace the horizontal line of reflection. Reflect this image horizontally.

1.
2.

187

That's the Point!

Mike arrives at the Oozma Kappa fraternity house with his suitcases. His suitcases are rectangular **prisms**, with **edges** and **vertices**.

A Complete the table.

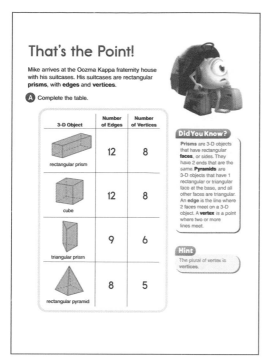

3-D Object	Number of Edges	Number of Vertices
rectangular prism	12	8
cube	12	8
triangular prism	9	6
rectangular pyramid	8	5

Did You Know?

Prisms are 3-D objects that have rectangular **faces**, or sides. They have 2 ends that are the same. **Pyramids** are 3-D objects that have 1 rectangular or triangular face at the base, and all other faces are triangular. An **edge** is the line where 2 faces meet on a 3-D object. A **vertex** is a point where two or more lines meet.

Hint

The plural of vertex is vertices.

188

B Use Venn diagrams to compare the features of different 3-D objects.

Hint

Compare features like number of faces, edges, and vertices. You can also compare whether the shape of the faces are the same.

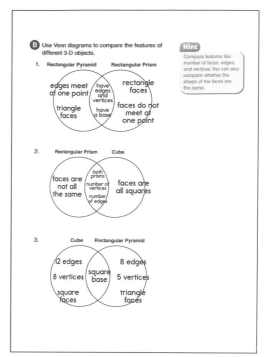

1. Rectangular Pyramid / Rectangular Prism

edges meet at one point / triangle faces / have edges and vertices / rectangle faces / faces do not meet at one point / have a base

2. Rectangular Prism / Cube

faces are not all the same / both prisms / number of vertices / number of edges / faces are all squares

3. Cube / Rectangular Pyramid

12 edges / 8 vertices / square faces / square base / 8 edges / 5 vertices / triangle faces

189

Building Boxes

Lightning McQueen's products are boxed and ready for sale. The boxes are rectangular prisms. They are built using nets.

A Match each prism to its net.

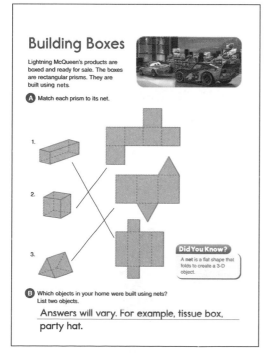

1.

2.

3.

Did You Know?

A **net** is a flat shape that folds to create a 3-D object.

B Which objects in your home were built using nets? List two objects.

Answers will vary. For example, tissue box, party hat.

190

On the Move

The toys are playing hide-and-seek in Bonnie's room. Help Woody find them using this grid map.

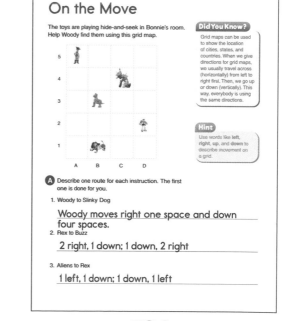

Did You Know?

Grid maps can be used to show the location of cities, states, and countries. When we give directions for grid maps, we usually travel across (horizontally) from left to right first. Then, we go up or down (vertically). This way, everybody is using the same directions.

Hint

Use words like left, right, up, and down to describe movement on a grid.

A Describe one route for each instruction. The first one is done for you.

1. Woody to Slinky Dog

Woody moves right one space and down four spaces.

2. Rex to Buzz

2 right, 1 down; 1 down, 2 right

3. Aliens to Rex

1 left, 1 down; 1 down, 1 left

192

Page 193

4. Woody to Buzz

__3 right, 3 down__

5. Woody to Rex to Aliens

__2 down, 1 right, 1 right, 1 up__

6. Rex to Slinky Dog

__2 down__

7. Aliens to Buzz

__1 right, 2 down__

8. Rex to Buzz to Slinky Dog

__2 right, 1 down, 1 down, 2 left__

9. Slinky Dog to Aliens

__1 right, 3 up__

B Woody wants to find each toy. Describe one continuous route that will take him to each toy.

__Answers will vary. For example, 1 right, 4__
__down to Slinky. Then 2 right, 1 up to Buzz.__
__Next, 2 left and 1 up to Rex. Finally, 1 right__
__and 1 up to the Aliens.__

193

Page 194

What Are the Chances?

The foreman at Monsters, Inc. does not know whom to choose for the next scare job. He could use a spinner.

A Examine the spinner on the right. Use these probability words to predict which monster will be chosen: certain, likely, unlikely, equally likely, impossible.

1. probability of choosing Orange Monster

__unlikely__

2. probability of choosing Yellow Monster or Orange Monster

__equally unlikely__

3. probability of choosing Red Monster or Green Monster

__equally unlikely__

4. probability of spinning Purple Monster

__impossible__

5. probability of spinning Orange, Yellow, Red, or Green Monster

__certain__

194

Page 195

B If you spin the spinner below 10 times, how many times do you predict you will spin a number less than 4?

Hint
To use the spinner, place a paper clip in the middle. Use the sharpened end of a pencil to hold the paper clip in place. Flick the paper clip to spin.

1. Use a probability word to describe the probability of spinning a number less than 4 in 10 spins.

__likely__

2. Spin the spinner 10 times. Record your results using a tally chart.

__Answers will vary.__

3. Did your prediction match the results of your experiment? Why, or why not?

__Answers will vary.__

195

Page 196

Sort It Out

The *papel picado* banners that hang in Miguel's village for *Día de los Muertos* come in many designs and colors.

A Sort each papel picado banner into the Venn diagram. Use the numbers beside each image to sort.

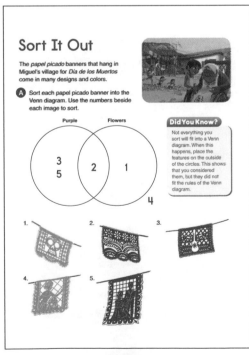

Did You Know?
Not everything you sort will fit into a Venn diagram. When this happens, place the features on the outside of the circles. This shows that you considered them, but they did not fit the rules of the Venn diagram.

Purple · Flowers

3
5 · 2 · 1

4

196

B. Sort each character into the Venn diagram. Use the numbers beside each character's name to sort.

Living ∩ Woman

4 5 | 3 6 | 2

1

1. PapáJulio   2. Mamá Imelda   3. Abuelita

4. Dante   5. Miguel   6. Tía Gloria

197

Label It!

The Legends practiced often for a race.

A. This **bar graph** compares the number of practice wins for each car.

1. Add labels to this graph.

Practice Wins for the Legends

Louise Nash: 5, Junior Moon: 13, River Scott: 7, Doc Hudson: 15

Answers will vary.

Did You Know?
A bar graph shows and compares information using vertical or horizontal bars. All bar graphs have a title, labels, and a **scale**. The scale in a bar graph tells you by how much each interval increases on the vertical axis.

Hint
Use the scale to find the value of each bar.

2. Who had the most wins? Who had the least?

Doc Hudson, Louise Nash

3. What is the scale of this graph? _2_

198

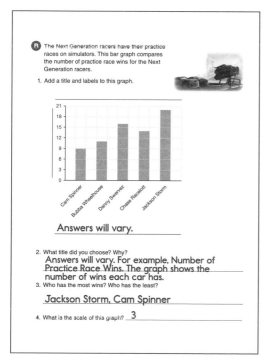

B. The Next Generation racers have their practice races on simulators. This bar graph compares the number of practice race wins for the Next Generation racers.

1. Add a title and labels to this graph.

Cam Spinner: 9, Bubba Wheelhouse: 11, Danny Swervez: 16, Chase Racelott: 14, Jackson Storm: 20

Answers will vary.

2. What title did you choose? Why?
   Answers will vary. For example, Number of Practice Race Wins. The graph shows the number of wins each car has.

3. Who has the most wins? Who has the least?
   Jackson Storm, Cam Spinner

4. What is the scale of this graph? _3_

199

Picture It!

On Monday, Dante collects 20 bones. On Tuesday, he collects 30 bones. On Wednesday, he collects 25 bones. On Thursday and Friday, he collects 15 bones each day.

A. Use the above information to complete the **pictograph**.

Title: _Number of Bones Dante Collected_

Monday 🦴🦴

Tuesday 🦴🦴🦴 🦴🦴🦴

Wednesday 🦴🦴🦴🦴🦴

Thursday 🦴🦴 🦴🦴

Friday 🦴🦴 🦴

Each 🦴 means 5 bones.

Did You Know?
Like a bar graph, a **pictograph** has a title, labels, and a scale. The scale in a pictograph tells how many items each symbol or picture represents.

200

201

B Draw a pictograph for the data below.

Shoes Made in the Rivera Workshop

Monday	8 shoes
Tuesday	12 shoes
Wednesday	10 shoes
Thursday	6 shoes
Friday	9 shoes

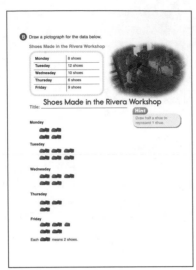

Shoes Made in the Rivera Workshop

Title: _____

Monday
👟👟 👟👟

Tuesday
👟👟 👟👟 👟👟

Wednesday
👟👟 👟👟 👟

Thursday
👟👟 👟

Friday
👟👟 👟👟 👟

Each 👟 means 2 shoes.

202

Interpret It!

Fans have packed the stadium to watch their favorite teams compete in the Scare Games.

A Read this bar graph about the number of fans at Scare Games events.

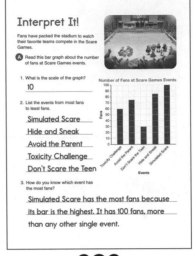

1. What is the scale of the graph?

   10

2. List the events from most fans to least fans.

   Simulated Scare

   Hide and Sneak

   Avoid the Parent

   Toxicity Challenge

   Don't Scare the Teen

3. How do you know which event has the most fans?

   Simulated Scare has the most fans because its bar is the highest. It has 100 fans, more than any other single event.

203

B Read this pictograph.

Number of Teams' Fans at the Toxicity Challenge

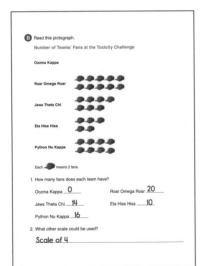

Oozma Kappa

Roar Omega Roar

Jaws Theta Chi

Eta Hiss Hiss

Python Nu Kappa

Each 🐉 means 2 fans.

1. How many fans does each team have?

   Oozma Kappa __0__   Roar Omega Roar __20__

   Jaws Theta Chi __14__   Eta Hiss Hiss __10__

   Python Nu Kappa __16__

2. What other scale could be used?

   Scale of 4

204

Graph It!

Bonnie has many different kinds of toys that she plays with all the time.

A Bonnie has 3 metal toys, 9 animal toys, 6 space toys, and 15 plastic toys.

1. Complete the bar graph to show this data.

Bonnie's Different Types of Toys

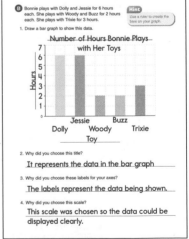

Toy Types

2. Why did you choose this title?

   It represents the data in the bar graph

3. Why did you choose this scale?

   The number of each type of toy was a multiple of 3, so it made sense to have a scale of 3

205

B Bonnie plays with Dolly and Jessie for 6 hours each. She plays with Woody and Buzz for 2 hours each. She plays with Trixie for 3 hours.

1. Draw a bar graph to show this data.

Number of Hours Bonnie Plays with Her Toys

Toy

2. Why did you choose this title?

   It represents the data in the bar graph

3. Why did you choose these labels for your axes?

   The labels represent the data being shown.

4. Why did you choose this scale?

   This scale was chosen so the data could be displayed clearly.

Congratulations

to

_____!

Print your name.

You have completed
this workbook.
You're a superstar!